FIRST CONTACT

Conversations with an ET

Tom T. Moore

Other Books by Tom T. Moore
published by Light Technology Publishing

The Gentle Way:
a Self-Help Guide for Those Who Believe in Angels

The Gentle Way II:
Benevolent Outcomes, the Story Continues

The Gentle Way III:
Master Your Life

Also available as ebooks

FIRST CONTACT

Conversations with an ET

Tom T. Moore

Cover art by Alan Gutierrez
www.alangutierrez.com

* * *

ISBN-13: 978-1-62233-004-1

Published and printed in the United States of America by:

PO Box 3540
Flagstaff, AZ 86003
800-450-0985
www.lighttechnology.com
For bulk pricing, contact publishing@lighttechnology.net

This book is dedicated
to all those who are seeking the truth
and reaching for the stars.

TABLE OF
CONTENTS

PREFACE

Since my last book was published in 2010, I've continued to ask hundreds of questions during my meditations. I had wanted to compile a book on my conversations with my own guardian angel, but the amount of work of combing through over five years of communications was daunting.

In 2008, my angel introduced me to a member of my soul group, or soul cluster. I've asked many question since. Then one of my weekly newsletter subscribers, Jim Connell, sent me a compilation of all the questions I had asked about these ETs, and I realized how easy it would be to arrange the many questions into chapter subjects. Synchronistically, I started to receive a flood of questions about these ETs. Events were conspiring for this book to come together. I even asked my guardian angel if this was the book I was supposed to write, and he said I was already behind timelines 7 and 8 (you'll learn about timelines in this book).

Besides Jim, several people helped with the initial editing and thematic arrangement of the material in the chapters. Special thanks goes to Helen Keahi, who edited several chapters, plus Antonia Witt, Rev. Dr. Carell Zaehn, Peggy Sealfon, Margaret Lubahn, Darlene Kirk, Teresa Austin, and Shana Holmes.

Thanks also goes to my freelance professional editor Ralonne Morss, who did the first read-through and who also edits my weekly newsletters.

I also would like to thank Melody Swanson at Light Technology Publishing and her staff, including my editors Barry Montgomery and Monica Markley. Light Technology has published all three of my books.

I can't forget my family, as we hopefully look forward to a great adventure coming our way in a few years. They have accepted the changes in the direction my life has taken since 2005. I still plan to publish a book on my conversations with my guardian angel, but my next book will probably focus on Atlantis, Mu, and Oz, as that material is quickly coming together.

INTRODUCTION

If this is the first time we've met on this journey we call life, then I need to give you some history of how I arrived at this point in time. You don't just decide to pick up the phone one day and ask, "Now what is that planet code?" to dial someone in another star system.

For me, it began in 1979 when I began recording my dreams each morning. Less than two weeks later, I had a very vivid dream of an explosion with a woman and some men somehow involved. My wife and I owned an international wholesale tour company at that time and had planned a trip to the World Congress of Travel Agents to be held in Manila in the Philippines. It was such a strong image that we canceled our trip to Manila and added days to stays in Taiwan and Hong Kong.

On the first day of the congress, terrorists exploded a bomb at the front of the hall where I normally like to sit, injuring ten people. An investigation found that four men were involved, along with a woman who worked in the Philippine trade office in the United States. I vowed then to record my dreams the rest of my life, and since then I've had other precognitive dreams, such as the Delta Airlines crash at the DFW Airport in the mid-eighties, the Challenger shuttle explosion on takeoff, and the 9/11 attack. But what was even more important was the discipline of remembering the dreams each morning, dragging them up from the distant recesses of my mind.

Most Benevolent Outcomes and Guardian Angels

About fifteen years ago, I began experimenting with requesting most benevolent outcomes (MBOs). I won't go into too much detail here, as that's covered pretty thoroughly in my first book. I will say it is the best modality I've ever found to reduce stress and fear and put you on an easier path in life. One of my subscribers to my weekly newsletter compared the law of attraction to driving an old Ford Pinto and requesting MBOs to driving a Ferrari — both may get you there, but the Ferrari gets you there a lot faster. You just say, "I request a most benevolent outcome for _____, thank you!" It's that simple.

What I did not understand at that time, and only learned years later, is that requesting MBOs has additional side benefits. It raises your vibrational level, which some people term "ascension." It keeps you on your soul path or "contract," which is the path you chose prior to birth for the greatest learning, challenges, and successes. As we are veiled from knowing our true soul selves, we have free choice in this life to choose whatever path we wish. Therefore, we stray off the path quite often. Requesting MBOs keeps you on the straight and narrow.

In 2005 my wife and I attended a seminar held in Sedona, Arizona, by Richard (Dick) Sutphen; it was designed to increase your psychic senses. I had attended a couple of his seminars previously and didn't feel I would learn much more; but my wife wished to attend, so I was there to support her. Was I wrong!

On the second day, Richard was going to put us into an altered state to give automatic writing a try. Previously Robert Shapiro, to whom I dedicated my first book, had channeled for me a Native American shaman named Reveals the Mysteries, who lived in the 1600s in the western United States. That's possible because all of our lives here on Earth are taking place at the same time, as time is an illusion (in a way, you can compare it to the movie *The Matrix*). I decided to try and contact him to ask why I was the major person promoting this fantastic modality of requesting MBOs.

After Richard put us under, I thought, "Reveals the Mysteries, are you there?" He responded, "Yes, I am." And I thought, "Wow!" I proceeded to ask him my question, and he responded by saying that I was a Native American shaman living in the same time period with another tribe. My name was Still Water, and I had decided to incarnate to live in the twentieth and twenty-first centuries to "reintroduce people to the Gentle Way." He said I was to "write books;" I resisted, saying I was just a business sort of guy, thinking that I would be continuing with my international film distribution work until I retired. He said, "No, books," very emphatically.

During the three months that followed this revelation, I wrote my first book using *The Gentle Way* as the title, which I had received that first time. I continued my conversations in what I would describe as a light alpha state. If you go too deep into the theta level, you really are not able to function to ask questions and write or type the answers. And when you come out of this alpha state, it is like waking from a dream. Soon you can't remember almost any of the answers — you have to read them.

Eventually, I started communicating with the being I believe is my own guardian angel. I asked him his name, and he said, "Oh, your vocal chords are not made to pronounce angelic names, so you can call me, Tom, Dick, or Harry, but Tom might be a little difficult in your meditations." I thought about it for a couple of weeks, and one day, the name "Theo" jumped out of my subconscious.

These beings are really old whole souls who volunteered for the work of overseeing all of our lives on Earth. There are a little over one million golden lightbeings — they emanate a golden light because they are so old and knowledgeable — taking care of all the souls having lives on Earth. I'll go into much more detail about this in my next book. I've since asked my guardian angel several thousand questions, many of them sent to me by my newsletter subscribers.

My angel says that he sends me thought packets. This is information that is filtered from the right brain to the left brain, and the interpretation a person of these packets is governed by his or her beliefs and knowledge. Later I learned that I've done this in literally hundreds of other lives, as he says I'm one of only ten people on the planet right now who have incarnated over 1,000 times. My angel states that the Gentle Way dates all the way back to a life I lived on the continent of Atlantis — what was left of it — about 200 years before it last sank into the sea. I was "inspired" to create the Gentle Way modality.

Why Tom Was Chosen as a Grassroots Contactee

As you'll read in the following chapters, I was chosen to be one of twelve grassroots contactees in 2017. Why was I chosen as one of the twelve?

First, you'll read how Antura, my extraterrestrial contact, and I are members of the same soul group, or "cluster" as my angel calls it. Each soul cluster has on average between six and twelve soul fragments. Our soul cluster consists of eight fragments having Earth lives. Naturally, communication would be easier between us. You could compare it to twins who know what each other is thinking, but in this case, it would be like twins on steroids.

Second, both Antura and I are from that same water planet in the Sirius B star system. I learned that I've had thousands of lives on that planet.

Third, I've been in the international film and TV distribution business for over thirty years, and have been involved in low-budget movie and TV show productions. You'll see where this plays an important part later in the book.

Fourth, my guardian angel is also the angel for Antura during his many lives on Earth, so it's easy for the two of them to communicate. My angel provides the questions he knows I will ask before my active meditation so that Antura can prepare.

Fifth, I have experience in receiving these "thought packets," which in a way is a form of telepathic communication — instantaneous across the universe with no time delays. I'm quite sure this will be used extensively in the future as we go out to the stars and must establish communications with the worlds we wish to visit. Each Earth starship will have one or more members of its crew who will be trained experts in this form of telepathic communication.

One thing I must explain. The rule for communicating with Antura was the same as it is for communicating with my guardian angel, or any other being with whom I now communicate. Antura is not allowed to respond to a general question about, let's say, his appearance or a detailed description of the mothership he will arrive in. I have to ask every single question regarding details. He can answer those.

A simple explanation is that this is the major difference between what I do in a light alpha-altered state and what a trance channel does when he or she steps away mentally and allows another being to take over and discuss a subject that being wishes to discuss. I'm given much more detail, but I have to ask the questions. Neither Antura nor the Angelic beings will provide answers for questions I don't ask.

The questions I asked span a period of five years. I compiled the questions into chapters on the same subjects. As an example, I might ask a couple of questions about the mothership one year, a couple the next year, and six months later two or three more. It would have been too confusing to list all the questions in chronological order.

Now for the story of how I was introduced to my "brother on another planet."

CHAPTER 1

MY FIRST CONVERSATIONS

The chapter opens on June 7, 2008. I was doing one of my active morning meditations, as I call them, asking questions of my guardian angel who I call Theo. Shortly after, on July 5, 2008, I began communicating with the extraterrestrial being Antura. These communications have continued on and off over the years, depending on my ability to think of questions to ask. Things really escalated after I decided to do this book instead of another I had been contemplating. Not only was I receiving more questions to ask from my newsletter readers, but my "writer guides," as my guardian angel calls them, were downloading a great many questions to me. The information provided from these sessions has been organized thematically rather than chronologically. An occasional symbol (✳ ✳ ✳) appears to represent a new session.

Someone channeled that between 2015 and 2025 we will know for sure of the existence of other extraterrestrial civilizations. Is that energy still in place, and if so, how will that come about?

An interesting question! Yes, they will begin making themselves known by then, as you will be at a higher level of vibration and spirituality, having learned secrets kept from you for hundreds and even thousands of years. It will make it that much easier for the governments to finally acknowledge that they have been in contact with these civilizations for many years.

Naturally, as you've read and heard, the process will be a gentle one with petite human-looking, nonthreatening peoples being the first to make contact. Certainly it will cause a sensation even under these parameters, but the beings who will come forward will have had much experience in these matters with first contacts on other worlds. They will make their existence known in the most gentle way possible so as not to frighten too many people.

Will it be in the United States first?

No, not necessarily. It may very well be in Europe.

What extraterrestrial civilization left artifacts of itself in Europe?

There have been several, if not many, that have left artifacts, but certainly someday artifacts from your Sirian neighbors will be discovered — but that will be just the start. They will be able to point these artifacts out to you at some future point.

When you said the Sirians would point out artifacts to "you," was that a general statement or me personally?

It will be you personally. You will have the privilege of meeting a Sirian one day.

That will be fun! Will I have previously known the Sirian I will meet in this life?

Yes, you will have known him quite well, and no, he is not a future incarnation of you. He is a friend, and yes, he will still be alive when you are born into that life.

So will he be on the planet I will incarnate on, or will he be on another planet?

No, he will be on the same planet. He wishes to greet you in this life to give you a glimpse of your next life. You will have a very nice chat. He will have answers to all your questions.

I hope he'll bring pictures of the world so that I can see them, since I'm veiled and can't recall what it looks like.

Yes, I'll mention that to him. [Pause.] He says that he'll be happy to.

So he's tuning in on our conversation?

Yes. You can speak to him if you wish.

I prefer to put together some questions first. What is his name?

That will be a little difficult for you today.

When an extraterrestrial visits Earth, how do they keep from being veiled too?

An interesting question. A complicated answer could result that is beyond your knowledge and comprehension at this time. Let's say that they have devices that act as a barrier to both the negativity of this planet that you're able to live with and any veiling that would try and cloud their memories.

✳ ✳ ✳

Antura

Is the Sirian's name Antu?

Fairly close.

My Sirian friend Antu — can you get me any closer to correctly pronouncing your name?

Hello. I am sending these thought packets to you and receiving you clearly. Antu is fine for the time being. We will get closer in the future, and I believe your computer will be able to adjust my name all at once, yes?

Yes, of course. I have not written down any questions, so I'll just ask them as I think of them. Please feel free to add information if you think I can receive more at this stage in my development in this life.

Yes, proceed.

Have you had any Earth lives before?

Yes, quite a few. We have known each other in both Earth and Sirian lives.

Then you are on the planet I will incarnate on next — is this correct?

Yes, quite so. I will be waiting for your birth with great anticipation.

How old will you be in my terms when I am born there?

More on the order of 400 years. Yes, that's close enough for today. I know you are still having a little problem with numbers, but that's fairly close.

I've been told that I will actually meet you in this life. Is that correct?

Yes, absolutely. It will be fairly soon, even in your terms. In the next few years, we will be allowed contact, and you're first on my list.

Will I just meet you and no one else?

That hasn't been decided yet. It will all depend on how you and the rest of the Earth people are progressing at that time period. We see things really picking up, although it is difficult to tell. Yes, there are still the wars and such with your country as one of the big instigators (even though it is not viewed that way). But soon things will turn inward due to all the financial and other problems brought on by hurricanes and also earthquakes.

Things will become much more peaceful, even though it would seem that you are opening the door for more conflict. It will be taken over, if you will, by the European Union, which will handle these matters quite satisfactorily.

Will there be any chance of a ride in your ship when you come to Earth or will that not be allowed?

No, you will be one of the first to enjoy that experience.

That's fantastic! I hope I'm not too old in Earth terms to enjoy the meeting, Antu.

No, not too old.

Will you be an ambassador to our world, or will this be a private meeting that is not publicized?

Good question. Yes, this will be more private. You will be told where to go to meet me, and we'll have a nice discussion — several actually — both aboard my spacecraft and in another suitable setting.

You don't speak my language do you, Antu?

No, I don't. Right now, of course, we are using these thought packets, as they're called, to communicate, but when we meet, I'll use a simple device we developed long, long ago for communicating with beings across the universe to translate what both of us say in an easy manner that will not be distracting to you. It is instantaneous in its operation.

You said I was first on your list, so when will you contact any others?

Soon after my contact with you. The other two will be prepared more as I'm preparing you so that you will not be frightened. That's another reason for what I hope will be many communications between us in the coming years.

Yes, I'm sure we will. Let's see about other questions. Do you have what we would consider some type of family unit?

Absolutely. I have my mate and children, although I am still considered young by our standards.

Do you want to try the age again with me?

More in the 450 to 500 range.

What work do you do?

I am part of the group that opens up or visits new worlds and assimilates them into this Federation of Planets.

Are you part of my soul group?

Yes, I am. That is a very good observation, or conclusion, shall we say. I was sort of sent on ahead to assist you not only in your present life but the next. We'll take good care of you, I assure you.

Gee, thanks, bro. Not sure how that translated back to your language, but here it means a close friend — like a brother.

Yes, it did translate that way.

How many planets outside of your solar system have you visited as part of your work?

Good question. A lot — certainly twenty to thirty.

Do you stay an extended time or a short time?

It varies according to what is needed. Most of my stays have been short to medium. We try not to be too obtrusive. We offer our assistance, make suggestions — very gently, shall we say — and then set up future meetings for others who have specialties needed by that particular people, as we shall call them, since they run the gamut from humanoids to other types of beings.

Then when you visit here, have you already started communicating with others?

Yes, but only one or two.

Okay, I guess that's all my questions for today, except for your name?

Want to give it a try?

Anturara?

Very close. Thank you, for your work. It will be quite important someday, these chats we are having. You'll see.

[Author's Note: I was finally able to get his name one day when I received the pronunciation An-tur-ah.]

Antura, how do you know on which days I will wish to speak to you?

It is quite easy. I receive this information in meditation, which as you know is much easier to accomplish than in the third-dimensional focus.

So with whom are you speaking?

My own spiritual advisors — they are not the same as your group of guardian angels, who are actually golden lightbeings. We do not need the same level of assistance you must have during your Earth lives, which are much more difficult than ours.

Okay, that's all I have for the present, Antura, unless I've missed something that you would like to discuss for a minute or so?

No, I must wait for you to come up with the questions, as they must be generated on your side as you develop more of an awareness and understanding and as you see gaps in what you have asked before. So I wish you a good life and a wonderful day too.

Before you go, why is it you are limited in what you can answer for me, yet a trance channel, let's say, can speak at length on a subject and answer questions?

A simple explanation would be that spiritual entities like myself can choose a topic of discussion, but in many cases, it must remain on somewhat of a general level. When they are asked questions, they are allowed to answer those questions just as I am allowed to answer yours. Then it comes down to how well they receive those thought-packet answers and how thoughtful the questioner is.

Plus, you'll notice there are subjects they will avoid or will give oblique answers to, or at times they will even say they can't answer the question asked. There are rules we must follow in our communication regarding explaining the operation of certain devices, shall we call them, as your scientists must invent those. We cannot give them the blueprints.

So, to summarize, there are the general topics that can contain a lot of information, which may not be completely understood at the time of transmission but will be understood in future years. And then there are those questions posed that we can answer directly but with limitations.

✳ ✳ ✳

Human Contact

Now I wish to speak to Antura.

Antura here. Arriving in a rush, would you say?

I didn't think you rushed at all, Antura, as it seems you are always relaxed when we talk. I'm the uptight one pushing to get in all my questions in a limited time.

True, but on this occasion, you decided to meditate even though you awoke late. It's one of those free-choice decisions that was not totally expected.

Sorry to throw everyone off today.

That's perfectly fine. It is my job to be available when you wish to speak to me.

Antura, when you prepare to communicate with me, do you already know the questions I'll ask beforehand?

Yes, for the most part, although if you recall, there are questions that you add as we cover a subject in more depth or as additional questions enter your mind.

So I assume my guardian angel apprises you of the questions?

Quite so. That way I can seek out information just in case it's not something I might not deal with on a normal basis.

When you rushed to speak with me the other day, did you retire to your house or to some other location?

No, to my house. Certainly there are public places to meditate if one chooses.

How often do you communicate with the other two people you plan to meet with during your trip to Earth?

Fairly often — more so perhaps than you. Their schedules are not so hectic as yours is, so they have more time and don't have the problem so often of tripping out — that is, going deeper into a theta state, as you've explained to your readers before.

What was my wife Dena's home planet. Was it in the Sirius B star system too?

No. She comes from the Arcturians — yes, you are receiving me correctly here. But her soul group was quite compatible with ours, so she has had lives with not only you, my brother, but with me too and with all of our soul-cluster members. That's the way it works, you see. We all mix and match.

Then will she be allowed to go with me on the ship?

Yes, if she wishes to. Do not force her to come, but I know you will do your best to convince her to.

* * *

Someone channeled that there will soon be no doubt there are extraterrestrials.

It will be a little longer in actuality, I assure you. There will continue to be sightings, but an actual appearance is not scheduled for some time. The sightings will be quite noticeable, and very dramatic — but no appearances of people, shall we say.

However, hundreds of thousands of people will see these flyovers, I'll call them, and they will not accept any government cover-up story. They'll say, "I saw it," and in many cases, they will also record it and download it to their computers. These accounts will be put up on websites, such as your YouTube and other social websites, as you call them, for everyone to view and comment on. That day is coming quite soon.

Since your days are not the same as mine, do you communicate with me at what are different times of your day, or are you able to be at the same time and simply work through the veil somehow. Do you do all of these question-and-answer sessions one after another?

Good question. Yes, I do meditate, as you call it, at different times in order to communicate with you. It is very important not only for you but for me and for my people that we establish contact and have more people know us so that there will not be such fear of us, since we are more different from you in appearance than, let's say, the Pleiadians. Knowledge overcomes initial fear.

Hopefully by the time I arrive, everyone will have much information about my planet and society. That is, of course, where you come in. That's why part of your job, or life purpose, is to open up these communications with me and perhaps one or two others along the way. So to answer your question again, I do these meditations or communications with you at different times, knowing a little in advance when they will take place.

How are you informed as to when I will meditate — which days and at what hours?

Ah, a good question. I am told this in my own meditation, which is easier here for us to accomplish than for you. So our higher self, or soul, lets me know when I should be available.

I'm glad we can communicate again so soon.

Yes, that is quite pleasing to me too. It assists in learning for both of us.

Why would races in other galaxies take such an interest in Earth to the point where it seems obvious that they communicate with people here, as you are doing with me? It would seem they would have many worlds in their own galaxies to concentrate on.

Yes and no. Yes, there are many other worlds, but none with anything like the experiment taking place on Earth right now. And now that you have successfully gotten over the hump, as you call it, there is much excitement throughout the universe about your accomplishment. That's why you've heard from your guardian angel that "parking is at a premium," as everyone has sent ships to observe and bring back knowledge of your accomplishments to their own worlds and galaxies.

[Author's Note: "Parking at a premium" refers to numerous comments made over the years regarding the number of spaceships from other planetary systems, galaxies, and even other universes researching planet Earth's human accomplishments.]

CHAPTER 2

ANTURA:
AQUA MAN

Antura, are you male or female or something else?

Yes, I am male. You did guess that already.

Could you pass as a human?

Not really, the differences are just too great. That's why you'll see people from the Pleiades first, as they are most like Earth humans and will not scare the general public. If we came first, there would be panic in the streets, as I believe you say.

Then do you live on a land mass or do you live underwater?

Ah, an excellent question. We do live underwater in large cities.

So are you a water being per se, or you can live on both?

Yes, both — quite so.

Do you have gills?

Of a sort, yes, although as you guessed, they are not noticeable.

I was going to ask this later, but describe your body. Are you slender as we would say?

Yes, we are of a slender build so that we can swim with ease.

How tall are you?

A little shorter than the typical Earth human but not much. Naturally there are slight varying degrees in our height too.

Do you have one skin color or are you different hues?

Our skin is a soft shade of blue with a little white and a touch of yellow. These colors help us blend in with our surroundings at an early stage of development, you see.

To a human's touch, Antura, would your skin feel rubbery, like fish scales, leathery, or like human skin?

It would be a combination but more rubbery and with skin — more like your dolphins, not like fish scales.

Is your head more or less round, or could it be some other shape such as an oval?

No, it is round but not as round as a human head. It appears more angular from front to back.

Does your head simply round off in the back, or does it come to an angular point of some kind — perhaps triangular or with a ridge running down the back?

No. It is smooth and round at the very back. When I said angular, I was referring to the sides and not the back.

Do you have nipples?

No, this is not something we have or need. Certainly our females do, but they are different from those on Earth.

Do you have any fins on your body?

No we do not, but that is a good question. We have very sleek bodies, shall we say, and fins would slow us down. Swimmers will especially understand what I mean when I say that over millions of years, we have developed the perfect body for swimming in the ocean.

Any body hair?

Not too much. Bald is beautiful — yes, that's a good old saying. Again, there is no need for body hair as there is for you humans. You have not found all the reasons for having body hair yet, but you will.

Fingers and Toes

How many fingers and toes do you have?

Four fingers on each hand — we don't have a need for thumbs, and we have four toes on each foot.

Are they webbed?

Yes, quite so. It allows us full movement in the water.

Are all your fingers the same size?

No, they are not. They vary in length just a moderate amount, but do keep in mind that they are perhaps a little longer than human fingers, as they are webbed in order to swim.

Do you have fingernails?

No, we have no need for fingernails as you do for protection. Your fingers have a habit of encountering many things requiring protection for the ends of your fingers. Our fingers do not.

Do you have joints in your fingers, and if so, how many?

Yes, we do have joints — two to three on average, depending on the length of the finger.

What about joints in your toes?

The same numbers as our fingers have, as they must be flexible for swimming.

You have stated that you have four fingers. Would one or more of them face the others in order to grasp or hold an object?

Yes. One of the fingers does oppose the others, yet not in the same way as the human thumb. It is offset just enough to assist in grabbing things.

Is the offset finger on the top or bottom of your hand?

On the bottom. This is completely the opposite of your thumbs, but there are reasons for this, as you'll see demonstrated.

It's not offset 90 degrees is it?

No, but it's difficult to describe.

Gills

Do you have a nose or just gills?

Yes, we do have noses and one set of gills.

Are the gills on both sides of your head behind your ears, or do you have just one set?

Actually, just one set. I know you thought I should have two, but we only have need for one set, sort of like having one mouth. So no, we are not like a fish from that perspective. My gill, using the singular name, is behind my ear, but normally it is almost imperceptible until I am in the water.

When you switch from the sea to a dry area such as your underground city, how do you switch from taking in air through your gill to taking in air through your mouths?

Yes, it is automatic with us. We don't even really think about it. The water is expunged from our gills, and then we open our mouths to breath. All in one motion, shall I say?

Are your lungs like air sacs?

Not in the way you have asked. Our lungs are completely different than yours. Again, they allow us to breathe at great depths.

When you are breathing through your gill, what intake are you receiving — oxygen, nitrogen, or what?

Good question. We are not oxygen breathers. We do take in a combination of substances, which does contain nitrogen and hydrogen, among others.

Do you breathe ammonia gas?

No, that would be harmful to our bodies. Here we get into an area you are not schooled in.

Eyes

What is the color of your eyes?

More on the black side.

Are your eyes elongated, or are they more round like the Zetas'?

They are more round but not to the extent of the Zetas'. More fashionable, you would say.

Do you use or have a second eyelid to protect your eyes underwater?

No, not in the way you asked. Our eyes are naturally shielded so that we can see great distances underwater with no transparent eyelids, just our normal ones.

Can you see in the dark?

Yes, our eyes can adjust to extreme darkness. It is quite a necessity in the depths of the ocean.

Teeth

Do you have teeth?

Yes, a fine set of teeth that are needed, especially in the early years, to tear seaweed apart for consumption.

So you do not have multiple sets of teeth such as some of our sharks and other sea life?

No, just one set is needed, and we now have devices to clean them, so we have no need for brushing as you do. A good question to ask!

Are your teeth flat or round? And how many do you have? Is the number different for females in your society?

Yes, they would look more round to you — we do not have incisors as you do for tearing meat. We are vegetarians, so the main use of our teeth is simply to chew various legumes that you would term seaweed. Regarding numbers, we have fewer teeth than do humans — typically less than twenty or twenty-two. And, yes, our females have a slightly lower count.

Organs and Body Composition

Antura, are you considered warm-blooded or cold-blooded?

Cold-blooded. It is necessary due to the depths of the ocean where we must live.

What is the color of your blood?

Red, but not the same color of red your human blood is — it is certainly a lighter shade.

Do you have multiple organs, such as more than one stomach?

Yes, we do have multiple organs — a couple, not including the stomach.

Would one of those be the heart?

Yes, we do have two of those. You are receiving me correctly.

Is the reason for having two hearts because it enables you to dive to great depths where you need a system to provide you with blood?

Quite so. We must have a larger capacity to pump blood at those depths, and having two hearts is really better than having one large one, as our chest would have to be much larger to contain one massive heart.

How does the rest of your body handle swimming to these great depths?

Good question. Our bodies are constructed more on the order of fish. You've seen videos or images on TV of fish swimming around deep within the ocean with no problem, and their molecular makeup is the same as in our bodies. Your scientists have done studies on why water pressure does not affect the fish swimming in your ocean, and one of them could explain this body construction in more scientific detail.

So although we are humanoid, our interiors, shall we call them, are extremely different from yours, as we have adopted over millions of years to living where we do, just as human bodies are built to withstand extremely hot and extremely cold temperatures. We could not. We would have to wear special suits — almost invisible to the naked eye.

Regarding the pressure of our oceans, yes, I would say it is similar, but not exactly the same, as our water is made up differently from yours. Again, this is something your scientists will find quite interesting to study one of these days — how your water differs from ours.

Do you have a rib cage similar to ours?

Yes and no. We do have rib cages, but they are different from the human ones.

How different?

A different bone structure and arrangement would be the best description I could give you.

Would the rib cage be located higher or lower on your body, Antura?

Let's say it extends just a little lower.

So just to make sure I got this right, your rib cage extends a little lower but has a different design, shall I say?

Correct. With a couple of different multiple organs, we needed to place them where they could be protected more in the earlier years of our existence.

Eating Habits

Do you eat the equivalent of fish in your world?

No, we have no need to kill our brethren for food. We gain all the vitality and energy we need from our plant foods.

Do you have a food source there that you eat that is also grown on Earth, and if so, is this a food source we already eat or one that we should look into eating in the future?

We eat a great deal of food grown in the oceans or processed from the ocean. And yes, that you also have on Earth, and it has even been studied, as it is quite common. But you have not discovered yet how to process this plant for it to be edible and an enjoyable source of energy for you. This will come in time as your scientists continue to study ocean plant life. I would not be allowed to give away all the information, as your scientists must discover this on their own, which they will do eventually.

Do you only eat vegetables from the sea?

Quite so. We can digest vegetables from the land, but much prefer those from the sea.

Do you have what we call stoves?

Yes, in a slight way, but certainly far beyond what you know. We just set the dial, so to speak, and our food and drink are delivered or created for us, depending on what we choose.

Do you need protein as we do?

Yes and no. Certainly there is a need for protein, just not in the amount Earth humans require.

Do you use any condiments on your food?

Yes, but not a lot. The vegetables we eat are quite tasty themselves, but certainly there are natural spices we can use to enhance their flavor if we wish.

What do you drink?

Besides water, pleasing blends of teas made from various forms of what you term seaweed. Obviously, these are various varieties of plants that grow profusely in our ocean and are cultivated, as I explained before.

When you eat, do you sit around some sort of table?

Yes and no. We have a variety of ways in which we typically intake our food. We may sit around on mats or pillows, we shall call them for your purposes; it is similar to how the Japanese people eat. There are counters and, yes, small tables, so there are a variety of ways we eat, but sitting on the mats is the most popular. Good question.

How do you clean dishes and utensils, which I assume you use?

Quite so. We are not barbaric, I believe the term is. Again we have these devices to simply insert the utensils and plates or dishes into and voila, they are cleaned instantly.

Ocean Living

How clear are your oceans? How far can you see?

Our oceans certainly would be even more pristine than the waters in your Caribbean, shall we say. We can see for thousands of feet — over a mile with ease.

How deep can you swim?

Oh, fairly comfortably at several thousand feet. Normally, there just is no reason to swim much deeper than the level that our cities are on.

How do you communicate underwater, Antura?

Certainly we have developed a number of skills in this department over millions of years. They range from hand gestures and mental telepathy to sounds we can emit underwater slightly similar to those of dolphins and whales on Earth. We use all of them.

It is my understanding that you did not begin on land first. Is that correct?

Quite correct. In the beginning, we began our lives in the ocean.

When or how long did it take you to become amphibian?

Quite a few thousand of our years. Our bodies simply adapted to where we could breathe on land and in the ocean.

So your bodies were not originally air breathers?

No, it took quite some time to reach that stage of development.

First Visitors to Antura's Planet

Did your first visitors from other planets in, I assume, the Sirius B system contact you in the sea or on land?

In the sea. Keep in mind there are other water planets in the Sirius B system, so they were quite capable of being able to contact us in the sea, although several thousands of years before we advanced as a society. Their religious leaders, shall we call them, made sure they began working with us at an early stage, as it was understood we would be bringing new blood to interact with these ancient societies.

Do you wear any coverings for your feet, either in your cities or on land?

Yes, a form of sandals in the city and more durable footwear on land, as yes, the ground can be quite hot. Although since our force fields handle all of this, we prefer a comfortable sandal.

Do you wear a hat or any protective clothing when you go on land on your planet?

We have not done so for several million years, not after we received instructions on how to build the force field. Before then, we had to be careful when we did go on land due to the heat. But to answer the question, we do not need to wear a hat or protective clothing when we go see our land brothers.

Were the land dwellers already on the planet when you arrived 18 million years ago?

Yes, they were. They were well established, but there was no real sentient life in the oceans. So we were invited, in a way, to settle there.

So do you have muscle groups similar to earthlings, or are they completely different?

Completely different, yet a few are similar — that's the best way to describe them. Naturally, being humanoids, we have to have some muscle groups the same, yet we have muscle groups dedicated to being able to swim.

I assume you have no reason to have gyms as we do on Earth?

No, not in the least. We get plenty of exercise when we swim, as we love to do that. When you enjoy something as much as we do swimming, then it is not a chore. Scuba diving enthusiasts on Earth will certainly understand these comments.

Length of Lives

Antura, how long are your lives?

We transition after 1,200 to 1,500 of your Earth years. We do not have the great challenges you have on Earth, so we can live longer and of course our scientific progress allows us to live longer than we would want to live on Earth.

Why is it that you transition after 1,200 to 1,500 years or so? Is it because your organs just wear out?

Exactly. Even though our bodies do not experience all the stress and disease your bodies do, eventually they do wear out, and it is time to transition and get a new body.

Do your people become frail with age?

Yes, the body begins wearing out, and we do move more slowly and swim more slowly as we near our transition point.

Egos

Do other beings, including you, have egos?

No. Not in the same way as you. Keep in mind that you're veiled and, therefore, the ego side of you is in control. We are much more centered, having full knowledge of our whole beings, so egos do not enter into the equation. That would be the best description I can provide.

So no other beings in the universe have karma or the need to balance as we do, is that correct?

Correct. No one else is veiled except Earth humans.

What vital life force powers your bodies? Are all your people fragments of whole souls?

Yes, they are. Their souls are capable of having several hundred thousand lives going on at the same time across the universe, so these are fragments of themselves. The life force comes from our own creators and, beyond that, the Creator of creators.

Does every being believe in a Creator of this universe?

We can't rule out that there might be some societies that do not, but overall, yes, they do. Again, they are not veiled as you are.

Aren't Creator, God, and All That Is simply interchangeable names?

Yes.

I guess that's all the questions I have for today, Antura. You certainly opened my eyes to the great differences there are between us. I trust we can work on that so that it will not seem so strange to me.

Of course. That's the purpose of these exchanges: to let people know about the vast differences just between humanoids, not to mention all the other forms of life in the universe. You will be amazed.

I hope you can bring photos or some sort of images of them when we visit in the future.

Yes, certainly I can and will.

CHAPTER 3

ANTURA'S PLANET

How long has your race been in existence?

Longer than you can imagine — millions and millions of years!

Have I had previous lives on this planet, and if so, why this particular planet?

The answer is yes to your first question. You have had a number of lives on this planet over the ages. You had lives here before your Earth lives, so you can imagine how far back in your time terms this would be.

Why so many?

Our soul group was attracted to this creation millions of years ago and started having lives here. It's the same attraction that causes souls to want to have lives anywhere in this universe. They are attracted to what they can learn and how they will learn it.

When was my first life on your planet — how many years ago?

Quite a few million, as you might imagine. Certainly over 10 million years ago.

Is it more than 10?

Oh, yes.

More than 20 million?

It's a little less than that, more on the order of 18 million or so, give or take a few years.

Where did our souls come from — another universe?

Exactly. We were created by another creator and were drawn to this universe. We had no physical lives in that universe before coming here.

About the Planet

Is your planet larger, smaller, or the same size as Earth?

It is a little smaller. Let's say, for your purposes, around 25 percent smaller. That's a close approximation.

Tell me a little about your planet. Does it have one or two suns?

Two, it's a binary sun system.

Does your planet have a day and night as we do, or is there no actual darkness since you have two suns?

There you have it. There is a time where the suns are not completely visible, so that creates the darkness.

Is this every day or during what we would call seasons?

Good question. Yes this is more during seasons as compared to a daily occurrence. My planet revolves at a slower rate than Earth, so it takes more time and seems to move at a slower rate.

Have we covered the rotation of your planet?

It is slower than Earth's. The days would seem longer to you.

How long are your days? Your city sits on the bottom of an ocean, I understand.

Yes, that's correct. Our days would be somewhat similar to Earth days, as we do allow for rest. Things are much easier here, so we have plenty of time to visit with friends, colleagues, and naturally, our families as well. So our equivalent clock would be more on the order of a twenty-eight-hour day.

Is your planet a water planet, just land surface, or a combination of both?

A combination. Ours is a vast water planet with some surface. I might've surprised you with that answer, but yes, that is the makeup of our planet.

Does your planet have icecaps during any time period?

Yes, but just a little at one point when the planet is facing away from both of these suns. And it lasts a very short time.

Antura, please describe the appearance of your planet from above. Is the water blue or green or some other color?

Yes, it's slightly different than you imagine. Sort of a bluish-gray.

What about the land?

Again, it's different. Not brown or green but more of a blue-green.

What is the percentage of land existing on your planet?

Before, I said it was much smaller than Earth. More on the percentage of 10 percent to 12 percent — you are close there. That percentage may seem small, but it does allow for some significant amount of land for those on our planet that are land dwellers, shall we call them.

Does the land on your planet have beaches or is it rocky or what?

Good question. The beaches are mostly covered with a rocky material, not too far from the look of your coastlines. There are some grainy, sand-like beaches on our world, but they are rare. There are also small coves that protect the land from water erosion.

Then the grainy substance that makes up your beaches would not be the same as anything on our beaches, is that correct?

Yes, there you have it.

Does the land on your planet have the same makeup as land on Earth, or is it completely different?

It is different, being composed of other substances and molecules and such. Perhaps it is similar to Earth's, but just not the same composition.

Then do you have such basics as iron ore?

Yes, but not in significant quantities. I would describe our landmasses as being more porous in appearance.

What are the colors of towns or cities on the surface, as you said there are beings who live on the surface?

Their form of living is quite different. From the air you would not notice their dwellings.

Atmosphere

What is the color of your sky above the planet?

It changes color due to the influence of the nearby stars or suns, as you call them. It can change from bright orange to yellow to a dark shade of blue as the suns circle around and we do the same around Sirius B.

Does your world have an atmosphere with wind and clouds?

Yes, it does have an atmosphere, although the clouds are nowhere near the same as on Earth, as they are made up of different elements from Earth clouds. They are more low-lying but still able to be seen. They have a similar appearance to the clouds of Earth. Billowy at times, especially when there are storms and it rains. There are winds, from what you would describe as a breeze to howling winds. Those on the land have structures that can withstand these winds, or they live below the surface.

I assume the atmosphere is not oxygen?

You are correct there. Certainly other elements make up our atmosphere — although you are having a bit of a hard time receiving these, as you do not have a scientific background. It is quite breathable for those who live on land and for us who live in the sea, you see.

Would this atmosphere be common throughout the Sirius B system?

Yes and no. Certainly several of the other planets have atmospheres that are similar but not the same, and then there are planets with completely different atmospheres. It is similar to the differences in your own solar system. And yes, ammonia is one of the elements, along with nitrogen, hydrogen, and other exotic elements.

I would assume you wear your protective device when you visit these other places?

Quite correct.

I'm told that, on Earth, we breathe in 79 percent nitrogen and 20 percent oxygen. Is the percentage of nitrogen higher on your planet?

Yes, it is and oxygen in much lower — less than 5 percent. We also have other elements that are higher.

Does that include hydrogen?

Yes, it does.

So does nitrogen act as a diluent on Earth?

Yes, to a certain extent, but that is not the only reason for this element to be in such a large amount. You need more of a scientific background for me to go further in this discussion.

The Surface of the Planet

What is the temperature on the surface and in the ocean?

As you may have guessed, the temperature varies quite a bit on the surface as it swings around and encounters the light from the Sirius A star. The temperature varies from quite cold to quite hot. The oceans, however, are able to absorb the heat and cold and remain fairly constant in temperature the deeper you go. That's another reason for having our cities deep in the ocean. They are not affected by temperature differences in the ocean closer to the surface. The land dwellers do have to adjust to the temperature changes that occur each year.

What is the temperature on the surface of your planet?

The surface varies greatly in degrees as we rotate around the Sirius B sun. There are times when the Sirius A star also is stronger as we orbit around our sun, so naturally these temperatures would feel boiling to you. That's the reason why the beings who live on the land do not have the same home structures you do. The temperatures range from quite freezing to almost boiling at times. This is why the land beings have thick skins and live in shelters to protect themselves from the heat.

What about the ocean?

Again, there is a great temperature differential from near the surface to down at the great depth of our cities, as you can imagine. The temperatures do not bother us at all. Again, we are made to live in an ocean and move freely about at any depth.

How deep in the sea is your city?

It would be the equivalent of one mile down — perhaps a little deeper than that.

Do you have ocean currents as we do?

Yes, there are currents in our ocean just as you have on Earth, but they are different. Yours are directed by the landmasses, but here there is much less land to divert currents. It would take an oceanologist quite some time to understand our varying currents, as they haven't even been able to figure out all the variants yet on Earth, although they certainly are on the way. But they have discoveries ahead of them.

What about underwater?

Except for the water near the surface, it remains at a cool temperature, although colder than your oceans.

On the surface of your planet, is the rain similar in composition to your ocean or as different as our rain is from our oceans?

Good question. The rains are similar in composition to our oceans. There are very small but significant differences in, shall we say, mineral content.

Is your water lighter or heavier than Earth's water?

It is somewhat heavier.

Would your planet's water be one-and-a-half, two, or three times the density of Earth's?

More than two times of Earth's, but less than three. It is still quite liquid, but just denser.

Is that because of the elements in the water or because there are molecules, say, closer together? I realize I'm on thin ice here with my lack of scientific knowledge.

A combination. It has more elements and a greater density in molecules.

Is the sea the same consistency, and is it heavier or lighter than our seas?

About the same but a little denser. The makeup of the molecules is slightly different.

Does it take much more effort to swim in heavier water than it would to swim in Earth's water?

Yes, but keep in mind that we have adapted over millions of years, so we have the strength to be able to swim in the heavier water. On Earth, we can literally fly through the water, as there is much less resistance.

This is not salt water as we have, is it?

Not in the least. The water's chemical composition is completely different from the salt water on Earth. That's the best way I can describe it for you, as you do not have a chemistry background.

About the City

Antura, how long has your city been in existence?

As I alluded to before, several million years. It is an ancient city by your standards. We do not tear down structures and cart them off to a trash heap, although that was done even here early in our existence. The structures are formed with the assistance of the planet and in agreement with the planet.

Are your spacecraft docked at your underwater city or on land?

You are correct in thinking we do have the capability to utilize these spacecraft both above and below the oceans. They act as both flying machines and submarines, you could say. So, yes, they do dock, as you call it, in special hangers for these craft adjacent to the city.

Is your city enclosed in a bubble, or is it open to the sea?

It is open in some places but primarily closed. We are equally at home in the sea or not, so we like to have it both ways, you could say.

Is your city dome-shaped, and is it transparent?

Yes to both questions. It is dome-shaped and transparent. We love to be able to feel as if we are in the ocean even when we are not. There was no need to protect our view of the ocean. On the contrary, we wish to see the ocean and all the creatures — the beings who reside there too, our friends.

What part of the city is dry, Antura, and how do you make the transition from ocean to dry?

Good question, and let's see if I can explain it. Certainly over 50 percent — perhaps a little higher — of the city is dry. We have many pools and entrances to the ocean, so you cannot say this part of the city is dry and this part wet. They are a combination, as our bodies need to be immersed in water quite often. It would be similar to your saying, "a fish out of water." It would be extremely uncomfortable to be out of the water for long periods of time. So we have water all around us in the city and even in our residences too.

Regarding how we transition from the ocean, it is quite simple: We have an airlock system. That's the best way I can describe it in your terms, where we easily pass through a couple of doors into the dry portions of the city. There is no waiting for pressures to equalize or that sort of thing.

How long can you remain dry, and should I ask in any temperature or should I say in your city?

Yes, while in our city, we tend to enjoy submerging ourselves several times a day. We do not really feel comfortable being away from water for long periods of time, but we can if we have our force field devices turned on. Then we receive the right amount of moisture for our bodies, so we are able to remain out of water for significant time periods. However, as soon as possible, we jump in the nearest pool, ocean, bathtub, or what have you. That's just who we are.

What material is your city constructed from?

Obviously, materials that are native to our planet. Stone and yes, various metals, some of which are known to you, but overall, they are quite different. I'm not avoiding the question, but explaining various metals that you have no concept of at this period of time would be rather difficult, if not impossible. Keep in mind that these metals were developed over millions of years, so they are quite complex in their cellular structure. The stone parts of some of our buildings are more for decoration, although in the caverns below the main part of the city, the cavern walls are sometimes used as part of a building.

Did your people first inhabit the caverns below the city and then build above over thousands of years?

Exactly. We inhabited these caverns for protection, and slowly built out, using the cavern walls as part of the structures we built. We then began building up and up over several thousands of years — a natural progression, you can say.

Does your city ever become dirty?

An interesting and somewhat amusing question. Yes, the city does need cleaning at times, but this is done quite differently by using robots. And keep in mind that the surfaces of many of the buildings and even interiors do not collect dust per se. Again it goes back to cellular structure. But to answer your question, parts of the city streets may pick up a little dust, but it is easily removed.

Do you have flowers and plants of some type and variety in your city?

Yes and no. We do have beautiful plants, but not the flowers you have on Earth. They have their own beauty and are cared for with great diligence and love.

Do you have any plants that would be the equivalent of trees?

No. There are only plants on the surface and none in the category of trees.

Do you have temperature controls for your buildings?

No, the whole city remains at a pleasant temperature for us, so there is no variance in temperature.

Then are there windows in your dwellings?

Yes, but not the same as you have in the United States. There is no need for window panes, so the windows are attractively molded, shall we say, allowing us to gaze out on our beautiful water areas of pools, fountains, and yes, waterfalls and flowing water. We are amphibious, after all, and we enjoy lots of water close by.

Do your cities have waste disposal systems?

Yes, they do, but far different from yours, as naturally there have been tremendous advances over millions of years, and the systems are so evolved that it is a little difficult describing them to you. Suffice to say everything is recycled and used for many different things.

Other Cities and Transportation

How many underwater cities are there on your planet?

Dozens. With a total population of 60 million, some of them are much smaller than yours. Our city is considered the central city, as we will call it for your purposes. There are several other cities that approach our size and then the dozens of smaller cities scattered all over the planet — not just in one region but all over.

Do you visit the other cities very often or at all?

My work is such that I'm not able to visit the other cities as often as some of our people do. It all depends on one's work, and some of our people must visit these other cities as part of their work. There are a few cities that would be considered more places to vacation, you might say, as they are located close to unusual underwater formations of various kinds.

Then I would assume you would use some sort of transportation if you do travel to these other cities?

Quite so, as you can imagine that even as fast as we can swim, the distances between cities would make it impractical. There are some who do this just because they have the time or inclination to do so.

Are these submarine-type craft, Antura, or do you travel through, say, tubes?

More the latter — yes, that's correct. The tubes allow us to travel at quite a high rate of speed while the underwater craft cannot even approach the speed of the tubes. Good question.

When you travel by tube, do you travel in some sort of vehicles — either singular or multiple cars — or is there a jet stream of water to propel you from one location to the next?

Good question. These are multiple-people cars; we will call them inside these tubes and operate them somewhat similarly to a subway system — just much more advanced.

What speed do they travel at?

Definitely in excess of your fastest bullet trains on Earth. They travel using a form of magnetism, so there is no feeling of speed, similar to that of our spacecraft — a highly advanced form of transportation.

What type of transportation do you use within the city?

Here it will be a little difficult to describe for you. We do have people movers, shall we say, but totally different from your people movers. It's as if we float on air, but in reality, we use a form of magnetics that propels us across the city.

Do they ever breakdown so that suddenly you can't float?

No, these devices almost never malfunction.

Energy

What source of power do you use to light your cities underwater?

Free energy, which you will soon be developing.

What are the sizes of the units that generate free energy for you? Do they vary in size according to their use?

Yes, these machines — or units, as we can call them — do range in size according to their designed purpose. Naturally, the largest ones are used to power whole cities.

How is this energy distributed to lights, machines, and so forth in your city?

There are no wires needed, and yet there are no harmful rays, either.

Is the electric current similar to the one we use?

Completely different. As you are not a scientist, it is difficult to explain this function to you.

Do you send particle beams to create light?

No, this is still something your scientists will have to create on your own. I cannot answer too many questions on this subject.

Communication

When you communicate with me, are you at a table, on a mat, or are you in a tank or pool of some sort?

A pool. I find it easier to connect while in a pool, so you will often find me here. That's why I had to rush back once before. I don't need to record these conversations immediately as you do. It's far easier to remember, so the pool is the perfect place for me to converse with you and everyone else.

How do you communicate across the city?

Certainly we have devices that can instantly communicate with anyone in the city we wish. We can even just think of the person we wish to speak to, and it automatically puts us in touch with them, if they are able to communicate at that time. We certainly can communicate as you and I are doing too, so there are multiple ways to communicate, including advanced video systems whereby the person appears in front of you and you're able to communicate your feelings on a particular subject.

Do you use both types of communication to confer with other societies, both on your world and other planets?

Exactly, but more on the side of the video systems, as communication with other planets is certainly more formal, involving trade and other governmental matters.

On your planet, Antura, how many other types of beings are you in contact with?

Quite a few. My water world is teeming with life, and certainly you will find as you progress that you are able to communicate on a feeling level with all sorts of species. They live their lives, just as we and you do. But there are times when problems arise. So we have people who are assigned to communicate our wishes or problems, and they do the same to us. We do have communication devices, don't forget; that makes this quite easy most of the time, although we are quite adept at feeling and compassion.

Money and Manufacturing

Do you consider gold, silver, and diamonds to be valuable?

Certainly, but not in the same way you do. They have uses beyond just being pretty to look at. You'll find many more ways these metals and gems are used in the coming years.

What does your planet use for currency, or are you a society that simply takes what it needs from one another?

Yes, in a way, we take what we need, but it is lovingly given. We contribute our services to our society. All members give what they can. There are none who are takers and not givers, if you understand my meaning. We don't have what you call unemployment. We all contribute to our society in most positive ways. There are certainly shops that specialize in certain goods, but again, we don't actually pay for these.

So was there a time when you used currency?

No, if a job needed done, someone always volunteered to do it if they were capable.

What is the work young people do on your planet in the water?

Cultivating the large amount of plants — what you term seaweed — is very enjoyable. It grows wild, but for a large population like ours, we need the Earth equivalent of farms, just underwater varieties. Then there is a form of processing. We don't just all go outside the dome and nibble on wild seaweed. That would last less than one day before it would be depleted.

What shops do you have and how are they compensated?

We have shops for such things as clothing. But again, as I have mentioned before, they gladly give these clothes out of love and mutual respect. The clothes are manufactured the same way — with love.

What do you barter with other planets?

There are elements we have in a water world that a very dry planet would not have but that are beyond your scientific understanding — and by that, I mean the understanding of your scientists here. There will be times when we will tell you to hold on to a resource because you will need it in the future, even though you have no use for it at the present time.

Do you pay for your dwellings in some fashion?

No, there are those who love to build and are pleased with us occupying what they have constructed.

Where do you obtain the basic materials to build your houses and manufacture your clothes, eating utensils, and so on?

We use materials mostly from our planet, although some materials we will barter for with other planets. It all depends on what we need to produce.

Do you materialize these things, or do you manufacture them?

Both. Certainly we have the ability to materialize almost anything, but there are basic materials that ask to be part of a structure, and they agree on a cellular level. We would never force them to be part of something they would not wish to be. Therefore, everything is made with love and respect. This is very advanced for

Earth people to understand, I realize, but you'll see what I'm speaking about in the many years of development ahead of you.

Do you have manufacturing companies on your planet?

Yes, small ones that manufacture what other planets wish to barter with us for. Most of this work is robotic in nature.

Tell me about what type of robots you have and for what tasks. Also, do you have androids?

Yes, a very good question. No we do not have androids. Certainly there are worlds that do utilize these beings, but we do not have a use for them here. We do have extremely sophisticated robots that perform a variety of menial tasks, along with very complex tasks that would be very difficult to explain at this time. There will be some robots on board the mothership when I come to visit you.

Sleep and Time

Are you aware of time underwater?

Certainly, we are aware more on the side of feeling when to eat and the light filtering down from above. We do not carry watches as earthlings do. We use feelings much, much more than Earth people do.

Do you follow a circadian rhythm that relates to light (sunrise) and darkness (sunset)?

Yes, in a way, as obviously light does not penetrate as far as a mile deep in the ocean. So, yes, our bodies can sense what we would term daytime, evening, or night. The lights in our city also adjust in a set fashion to remind us.

Since you live under the sea, how long is your day or the time period you are awake and working and so on, or do you sleep?

Yes, a good series of questions. I'll take the last one: We do sleep. Not as much as Earth humans, since we do not need to, but yes, we do sleep and dream. As you have asked before, most beings in the universe do dream.

Our days would be considered long to you — twenty waking hours or more would be the equivalent. As these days, we'll call them, are not as stressful as on Earth, we are able to be awake and work and play and study and so forth for longer periods of time

Do you sleep in water, Antura?

No, not exactly. We sleep in more or less dry conditions, but again, water is close by if we feel dehydrated.

Undersea Inhabitants

Antura, you mentioned dangers when your people first arrived on the planet 18 million years ago. Was that from flesh eaters both in the sea and on land?

Quite so. There are still a few dangers we avoid when swimming, shall we say. They are quite well known, and it is easy to avoid them — and, yes, that includes flesh eaters.

Would these flesh eaters be shark-like, fish, or what?

More on the order of a flesh-eating whale, large creatures who require a lot of food. We avoid them like the plague.

What else does the flesh-eating whale eat? I would assume large quantities of the fish species you have?

Exactly. They must go after large schools of fish to satisfy their craving for food.

Do you communicate now with those large whale-type, flesh-eating creatures in your ocean?

Yes, but on a very limited basis, as they are simple creatures who must spend every minute of their time foraging for food due to their large size.

Are there any fish in your oceans that are similar to Earth's fish?

Quite so, yet different. You have an enormous number of species, so they are quite similar in nature to ours, at least your more exotic ones.

Are there equivalents to our seals and other water-based animals?

No, our animals are not the same. Certainly we do have some water-based animals, as you term them, but they would be considered more developed than those on Earth.

Do you have coral reefs as we do?

Yes, but they are quite different, as the sea life is quite different. Therefore our reef system is different, but it is very beautiful. Naturally, the reefs also play a part in our currents beneath the surface.

Surface Inhabitants

What about the plant life and other life forms on the surface of the planet, Antura?

This is a little hard to describe, but there are a number of exotic plants both above and beneath the sea. Some have brilliant colors while others are a little drab by Earth standards. We do have other land-based beings on the planet.

They are not humanoid, are they?

No, they are not. They look quite different.

Are they four-legged?

Yes, some are and some are not. It is not just one type of being; there are several.

Are there bird beings?

Yes.

Would any of these be insect or reptilian?

No reptilians, thank you, but yes, we do have some insect beings on the planet. Again, there is some variety, but not nearly the variety on Earth. We have pleasant dealings with all of them.

Are they all as advanced as you?

Yes and no, again. Certainly we can communicate with them all, but we allow them to progress at their own rate, and some desire, shall we say, a simpler life.

You said that you have no other humanoids on your planet except yourselves, is that correct?

Yes.

Describe the birds.

There are waterfowl, you might call them, plus some other bird creatures that inhabit the land masses.

Are you able to communicate with them?

Yes, but on a lower level. Keep in mind that we have the capability to communicate with almost every creature in the universe. We have developed these capabilities over millions of years as we branched out to the other worlds in our neighborhood, shall we say.

CHAPTER 4

ANTURA'S FAMILY
AND FRIENDS

Antura, how many people did you say live on your planet?

No more than 60 million. That is a nice number that gives everyone plenty of space.

How many people live in your city?

Actually, less than one million. I know you thought perhaps it would be even smaller than that, but we have a fairly large city that was built over a very long period of time that expanded many times, as you can guess.

So would there be more than 750,000 people there?

Yes.

But less than one million?

Yes, but just slightly less.

Do you live in the fifth dimension?

Yes, that's correct there, you see.

Where did your people originate?

They came from — their souls, you know — from another creation, as they were drawn by the Creator of this universe's variety and plans.

Were you water beings before becoming amphibians, or were you always amphibians?

In the beginning, we were water beings, but we developed over time into amphibians. It was simply an adjustment to our living conditions. We enjoy ourselves and have great pleasure in the water, but we also can and do spend time on the land — although, it must be near the water for us to do our meditations and such. We tend to stay close to the ocean when we do venture out to visit the land beings that inhabit our world.

Quite so. Yes, they must live underground in caverns and places they have hollowed out, due to the changing temperatures as we rotate around our Sirius B sun and also at times face the Sirius A giant sun. So their lives tend to be underground.

How large a population do they have?

Several million, not as large as ours. Perhaps their's is half as large as our population. Don't forget that their landmasses are smaller than those on Earth.

Does every soul on your planet at one time or another have lives on Earth?

No. This is interesting, as there are souls with no desire to become caught up in the Earth Experiment. They are not forced to, you see. So that's where you and I can make a difference, as we can bring back ideas on improving our world.

Manners of Living

How do you typically spend your day?

Naturally, I start with my mate and children, you see, and then meditation. Then I will work — not necessarily at any particular building or center, although I will do that on occasion. Many of my studies are done right where I am, along with reports that would be considered very complex to you at this particular stage — especially if we have just returned from visiting another new planet that we have not had contact with before. I will also take time to visit with friends and colleagues, if you will, to exchange ideas and so forth. Perhaps that sounds similar to you in a way, but it is also quite different, as you can imagine.

Antura, just to have a snapshot of your life on your planet, what were you doing when my guardian angel notified you that I was meditating?

Not so much. I was conversing with my friends at a local bath. As you know, we do like water, and it gives us pleasure to enjoy our friends' company at the same time.

What is your formal greeting and then the one for your friends?

We greet people — other beings — in the manner they are accustomed to. We are quite adaptable that way. Among our own friends, we embrace and there is a special touching of hands.

Do you just wear a toga in the city?

Quite so. Dress is casual in our cities.

What color toga do you wear, and does it cover you from the waist down or shoulder down? And what about trim?

Yes, the togas we wear are more from the shoulder and can come in many colors, just as your shirts and slacks of this time period. I prefer blues and greens, and our togas come with various trims and designs. They are not just some plain linen cloth but reflect our moods, as does your color selection on Earth.

What about when you visit other worlds?

We tend to dress up a bit, as I believe you say, with finer clothing. Sometimes it is similar to the clothing of the people or beings we are visiting. The clothing and designs are more intricate, as we do have a more formal attire should the situation demand or require it.

How do you clean your garments?

We are well past the point of washing machines, so there are devices that instantly clean any garment we have. No fuss, no muss, you could say.

Antura, do any of your people use astrology?

Not like Earth people do. Astrology was presented or given to you as one of the tools available to assist you through life since you're veiled. In the ocean, we are more protected or blocked from various astrological aspects.

Do you have some sort of calendar?

Not like you do. We do not count time as you do. It's not important to us, you see.

Are there healers on your planet?

No, not in the same sense. Certainly if there are injuries, we have many ways to treat the patients — from healers to specialized equipment. Injuries are healed immediately.

Then do you have doctors or just people who are healers?

No doctors per se. Just people who can attune with a person's body.

What form of government do you have?

It is a form of democracy but much less structured than your own forms of government on Earth. Naturally, we do have citizens who enjoy that type of work, as far as keeping a large city running and communicating with the other cities and villages on our world. There is very little that goes on in comparison to even one day or one week on Earth. We do not have the challenges you do.

Are there any challenges your species faces right now, and what are you doing about them?

There are no major challenges facing us at the present time. We have had millions of years to overcome any challenges we faced. Our major challenge coming up in a few years will be the introduction of negativity by Earthlings, so that will result in major changes for our society.

Do you have artists, and if so, what kind?

Yes, certainly we have artists who create, although not in the same ways as you do. Even art has progressed over millions of years, and what they work with now is completely different from what artists use on Earth. It is very difficult to describe in three-dimensional terms.

What about musicians?

Certainly we have a number of our people who are musicians with locally produced instruments, some that would be similar to what you have — flutes and such. Again, there was progression even here, and the instruments that they play are quite advanced.

Is swimming your recreation, or do you have other physical activities?

Yes, we obviously do love to swim, and that is our recreation.

Besides swimming, what is your entertainment?

In past sessions, I have mentioned that we do have music and we have discussions with friends, a bit similar to the ones you might have with your friends. We have a wealth of information at our fingertips about not only our world and star system but any star system across the universe. It would be the equivalent of having your National Geographic and history and space information TV channels all rolled up into one.

So you don't have games as we do, or do you?

No, we do not. That will be one of the things you'll probably introduce us to — "you" meaning humans — when you start visiting all your neighbors, uncles, and aunts, so to speak.

Do you, as a society, ever put on plays on your planet or on the mothership?

Yes, there are lighthearted plays presented as part of our cultural enjoyment. And, I will add, we have our own versions of televised dramas too. They are not of a class that your producers and directors are doing on Earth, as we abhor violence, so again, these are lighthearted, amusing productions.

Other than swimming and get-togethers with friends, are there any other leisure activities you have that we have not covered?

Of course, we have covered plays, reading, concerts, and just strolling through the city.

Does your society have stimulants of any kind?

Yes. There are certain seaweeds that contain stimulants — we will use your term — and we can make a juice from them or eat them.

Are they used all the time or only on special occasions?

Most of the time, let's say for your purposes, we use them when we are with friends.

Personal Relationships

Have I asked what your mate does?

No, you haven't. She does have her work too, but it is completely different from mine. It would be a little difficult to explain at this time, but it has to do with the government.

Has she had lives on Earth before too?

That's an excellent question. Yes she has, so certainly that drew us together, as we have had lives on Earth together before, so there was instant recognition. Even if we had not had lives together, the fact that we had Earth lives tends to join our people together as our auras and outlooks and so on are similar.

How many lives on Earth has your mate lived?

She is a little behind you and me. Yes, she is more in the 600 range; that's much closer to the number. Still, that is a lot of lives, which is why we get along so well together. She is a seasoned soul in Earth lives.

Have you or I ever had any lives on Earth with your mate?

No. Neither of us had previous lives with my mate, but that is a good question. Her path was quite different from our own.

Anything more that you can tell me about your mate's work?

Not a lot. It has to do with things that are not even on your drawing boards yet, so it is difficult for me to describe something far beyond your understanding at this time.

Antura, how many years is a typical relationship on your planet, or does that vary as widely as ours does?

Yes, it does vary, but I would say our relationships — meaning mating in this case, since that's how I understand your question — could be 500 years on average. That would be an average, and certainly there are those on our planet who live together for a much longer time.

Do you periodically change mates?

Yes, we do periodically change our mates as we grow or go through stages of our lives. We all remain friends, and children are always welcome in our dwellings with the new mates. This is, after all, a much easier existence without the great turmoil encountered in Earth lives. We are a big happy family, for the most part.

Please explain about your mate selection and courting.

I'll try. Again, when we meet someone, it is much easier for us to identify them if we've known them in one or more past lives. We are not veiled as you are. Therefore, we can identify them from feelings, from auras, and from our meditations to see how far back we might go. Then it is a matter of hooking up, shall we say, in which we introduce ourselves and begin to talk about ourselves, our work, and so on — families. It's just a natural progression. Again, it is this instant recognition that is much easier to identify than it is on Earth, where you are veiled. Over a short period of time, we explore our compatibility and decide if we should mate.

How can you tell if someone is not mated?

Yes, it is an instant recognition developed over millions of years. We do not have the equivalent of the rings that you have, but you can tell just by the emanations that they are single.

You say that you see an aura around a potential mate, then is everyone on your planet able to see auras?

Yes, everyone is able to see auras. This is pretty natural after such a long time. Many more people on Earth will be able to see auras after your jump to the fifth focus.

Does your aura appear different since you have had 800 lives on Earth?

Yes, actually it is quite different. It is more colorful. Naturally, we do not particularly concentrate on another being's aura, but again, it is easy to switch our focus to view another's aura if we wish.

So it is more colorful because of your many lives on Earth?

Exactly — a coat of many colors. I believe there is that saying on Earth.

How old are your females when they can reproduce, and do they have periods as women do on Earth?

Yes and no. Our females are able to reproduce at a later age, as it is not necessary to reproduce as young as Earth females do, due to your shortened age or life span. They typically do not reproduce until after their 125th birthdays. That figure you have is very close. There is no pressure on them to reproduce, as compared to the much harsher conditions on your planet. Many of these females do not reproduce for quite some time after that — again, they are not rushed but are able to enjoy their youth without the pressure of raging hormones that young women and men have on Earth. Regarding periods, they do not have them until they wish to reproduce — that's about the easiest way to describe it.

How do you conceive children — through sexual intercourse or by other means?

This is perhaps slightly difficult for you to understand at this time. We do conceive but not by artificial means or cloning. We do have sexual intercourse, and it is a very spiritual experience with greatly cherished feelings of the moment.

Do the males have penises and the women vaginas?

Yes, although not like the ones you have on Earth. They're different, but again, it's a little difficult to explain.

It is reported from some planetary societies that the males have the ability to retract their penises. Is that the same for your society?

Quite so. I knew you would get around to asking this. Certainly it is not only for protection as we swim in sometimes dangerous waters, it also allows us to swim faster, with less drag on our bodies, and it also makes it easier to appear in public without a toga should we so wish. There are other benefits internally, but those are some major reasons we have developed this way.

Do your females have retractable vaginas?

No, not in the way you are thinking. When we have sex — which, as I explained, is a very special event — the female bodies change with the vaginas, let's say, dropping down would be the best way to describe it for your purposes. It is sort of the opposite of what you imagine.

I assume birth takes place in the water?

Oh, quite so. We are, after all, water beings. Again, it's a very loving experience without any pain of birth as you are accustomed to.

Are your babies born with umbilical cords?

Yes, they are — not so much different from an Earthling birth in that aspect.

What about the female breasts? Do they have breasts, or is this something only noticeable when they are pregnant?

There you have it. They enlarge in a similar way to human breasts, whereas normally, they are not noticeable, as compared to the wide range of women's breasts on Earth.

Do your mothers breastfeed, or are your children able to immediately begin eating vegetation?

No, our mothers do breastfeed for a few weeks until there is growth. Then small amounts of tasty vegetables are introduced to wean them away.

❋   ❋   ❋

Children and Schooling

Good day to you, Antura, and good life to you and your family.

Many thanks. Yes, they are doing well, my little tadpoles and my partner.

How many children do you have?

Two children.

Male and female or two of the same gender?

Two males.

How are they schooled, and for how long?

Our school system is totally different than anything in your conception. We have pods for learning, and they spend time inside the capsules and learn at a very rapid rate. The information is fed directly into their brains according to the interests they have. Their interests are determined by what we will call their DNA profiles.

It's my understanding that you do not have a school system per se?

Correct, although there are centers where specific knowledge is kept, and anyone has access to these, including our youngsters. They also use these skull-type devices we have spoken about before to download great amounts of knowledge about specific subjects. Again, it all depends on the child's interests.

How long do children study each day, or is everything given to them mentally?

Another good question. They do have these emersions, shall we call them, where a great deal of information is downloaded through the skullcaps. This is done in a fairly rapid manner, so plenty of time is left to discuss the information with their classmates and instructor-facilitators, shall we call them. They are simply there to clarify the information they have received and expound on it, if necessary.

What do your children do for fun? I assume they do have play activities.

Oh, yes. They have great fun with other children swimming around our city and exploring and getting to know the sea life. This is considered most enjoyable to our people, and there are many places for them to swim and enjoy the sea. That is their primary enjoyment, along with being with other children their age. They are quite active between their times to study.

At what age were you taught to pilot any sort of spacecraft, or is this something simply downloaded into a child's brain?

After the information is learned, or downloaded — and this does not happen early in a child's life, since there is no pressure to do this — the child must want to learn. Many have no interest in learning. After the information is downloaded, the children take a short course in piloting the craft — hands on experience, if you will. This can come at any young age, say from ten or twenty years on up to fiftyish. Again, many are quite content to simply live and eventually work in the sea and have no interest in going to a nearby planet.

Do your children grow fast, or do they mature more slowly than Earth children?

Certainly, as we live much longer than you, we can mature at a slower rate. However, because of our technological advances, information is readily available as our youngsters are ready to absorb it. We just allow them to go at their own pace and learn what interests them. And I might add that there is so much to explore that their minds are never in neutral.

Do you take your children and mate to other planets with you, including new ones you are contacting for the first time?

No, not the ones we are just contacting, as this can take much time. They have gone with me to neighboring planets to see other cultures, just like you take vacations on Earth.

Celebrations, Ceremonies, and Customs

Are there any specific religions on your planet?

Yes and no. The religions would not be the same as yours. They are much gentler, shall we say, than yours. There is the acceptance that there is a Creator of our entire universe, yes. Then there are some ancient rituals that have been handed down that are performed from time to time — not every few days but on special occasions. This goes not only for our people but those who live on the land.

Do you celebrate birthdays or anniversaries of, say, when you mated? What days do you celebrate?

There is the day each year when we celebrate the union of the planets in the Federation. It is fairly low-key. Birthdays, except for the very young, are not celebrated much due to the length of our lives. Anniversaries with our mate also tend to be low-key. We might take a swim together.

We do have spots that serve as gathering places where we can relax with friends and have a bit to eat, but they are not like the restaurants you have on Earth. They're quite different. Life here, as you can imagine — or perhaps cannot imagine — is totally different from life on Earth.

Do you have any sort of ceremony when you mate or any sort of requirements to officially be together?

No, there is no need for an official ceremony as you have. We are able to feel the attraction, and after a time of courting, we decide to live together. It is not a situation in which we go jumping from relationship to relationship, as we can feel the other's vibrational level and whether it is compatible with our own.

Is there a celebration of mating or bonding together?

Yes, but it is rather low-key by Earth standards. Certainly our family and friends get together, and there are certain ancient ceremonies we partake in that could be described as wishing love and happiness for the couple.

Antura, please describe your funerals or memorial services — or do you have any?

Oh, yes. We have services that date back to ancient times whereby we honor the passing of our family members and friends. As we are quite aware that the soul is no longer attached to the body, the body is taken out of the city and into the sea, just as it was done in ancient times. It is gently placed in a special spot and left there for the sea to take back. Yes, it is a solemn occasion, but back in the city, the memorial, we shall call it, is more of a celebration of our loved one's life.

Is the body placed on some sort of rock or just on the ocean floor? Is it dropped into the depths of the sea?

More on a promontory overlooking the deepest part of our ocean.

Meditation

Can you explain more about meditation in the water and on land?

Perhaps just a little more. We can hold ourselves motionless in the water, just floating while we meditate. It is a suspension, if you can imagine. We do not meditate very much on dry land, as we cannot attain the same sensation we do in the water.

Is there a group called the Sirian High Council residing in lightbodies in the sixth dimension?

Yes, there is that group, along with others that exist in that dimension too. We gain guidance from them through our own clergy, if you will.

CHAPTER 5

ANTURA'S
STAR SYSTEM

Antura, is your planet in the Sirius star system known as Orion?

No, it is not. The Orions do inhabit another planet in our star system, but we are not them, shall we say.

Are there more or less twenty planets inhabited in the Sirius B system?

Yes, a little more — twenty-one, let's say for now. Very close.

To verify a previous question, Antura, how many planets are there in your star system?

Over twenty. Quite a large number, which is why there is much interaction between us. There were just so many planets with life on them. It was only a matter of time until one race after another developed the capabilities of interplanetary travel. As they saw the other planets were peaceful, good trade resulted.

What beings inhabit them?

Of course, there are many types of beings on those planets, certainly not all humanoid. Over the centuries, we'll say, this gave us much to work on — coexisting with all the many different forms of life so very close at hand — compared to your situation, where by design it appears there is no other life in your solar system. It's all part of the experiment.

How many planets in your solar system are inhabited by humanoids?

Approximately half — a little more than that but not much.

Give me some examples, if possible, of nonhumanoid intelligent beings, whatever that definition means to you.

Yes, there are some really different beings, including an otter-like species. Then there are water beings, which equate to your dolphins and whales, and a glossy luminous creature that has no specific form. There are also some animal-looking creatures of high intelligence. There is quite a variety.

Have you encountered the beings in the Sirius system who are able to run and jump and fly on wind currents around their planet, as described in Robert Shapiro's Animal Souls Speak *book?*[1]

Oh, yes. We are quite familiar with these lovely people. As you have read, their primary sustenance is a fruit found only on their world, so their travels are quite limited.

They will not be with you when you come?

No, they will stay on their home planet. They have a very peaceful existence, and their main contact with you is to ensoul the manta rays in the sea, or as they call them, "birds of the sea." This was of course asked of them by the Creator's emissaries.

How many water planets are there in the Sirius B system?

There are six; that is the correct number.

Are there any in the Sirius A system?

Just a couple.

Does the Sirius B sun, which we know as a white dwarf, emit a constant source of light?

Yes it does.

Does the Sirius B star shine white, or does it have a blue appearance?

No, the light from this sun has just a light-bluish tint to it, which obviously gives a slightly different appearance to our planet.

What about the sun we know as Sirius A? It's huge! Do you orbit far enough away from this sun so that it doesn't have a huge impact on your surface and the surfaces of the other planets?

Yes and no. Some of the planets orbit closer to this sun and certainly are much hotter than my planet. It's good that you thought of that. And yes, that's why those who dwell on those planets must have very thick skin in comparison to ours and to your Earth human skin in order to survive a much hotter existence. Their bodies did adjust to these conditions over millions of years. Farther away from the sun, those surface dwellers do not need such thick skin, but their skin is still thicker than yours or mine.

Is there a sun also revolving around Sirius A called Sirius C?

Yes, but farther out and it does not affect us too much, you see.

How many days does it take to make it around your Sirius B sun?

It takes a lot longer time to circle our sun than it takes Earth to orbit its own — and don't forget the influence of the Sirius A sun. Certainly we can say twice as long.

---

1 Robert Shapiro, *Animal Souls Speak:* Explorer Race Book 13. (Light Technology Publishing: Flagstaff, 2007.)

Is your planet the third from the Sirius B sun, or where is it located?

Yes, its orbit is the third from the sun, as Earth's is.

Antura, for the Sirius B star system, would the numerical population of the society on your planet be considered average, above average, or below average?

It would be considered a little below average. I know you have been reading information from other channels who communicate very small populations, but the reality is that most societies, at least in our star system, have much larger populations.

How long have the oldest societies in the Sirius B system been established — over a billion years?

Yes, even longer than that. A couple of the societies you would consider, as we do, to be very ancient — several billion years. I know this is hard to wrap your mind around — I like that saying — but they are a loving people and our good friends and mentors, you could say.

Are you able to breathe underwater without a device on Earth and on the other water planets in your system?

Yes. Our gill structure allows us to separate what we need in all but one or two planets. On those few planets, the water is so polluted, shall we call it, with heavy elements that our gill structure cannot cope, so we must use breathing devices. We need these devices to protect our bodies from these heavy elements, as they are quite acidic in composition.

Was the water on these couple of planets polluted by beings, or was this water created that way?

They were created and not debased or polluted by beings living there. Naturally, when the Explorer Race begins to explore the universe, the Sirius B system will be one of the first ones visited, along with the Pleiades. We will give tours of all the planets to show the differences in each one, including the two with heavy chemicals and metals in their waters. There will be great learning in what will be considered a fairly short amount of time once you get to the point of traveling to the various star systems yourselves.

Contact with Other Planets

How long after we started to have lives on your planet, 18 million years ago or so, did your neighbors start to call?

Certainly we had developed to the point at which we had a society and clustered settlements, shall I call them. To answer your question, it was long before we reached the point at which we wanted to see what else was out there. But that really spurred our development.

Did your society's first contact with another planet involve one in your own star system or one outside of your system?

Good question. It was a planet in our star system, and yes, they contacted us first. They were much more advanced at that stage than we were, and they precipitated the contact.

Did your first visitors from other planets in, I assume, the Sirius B system contact you in the sea or on land?

In the sea. Keep in mind there are other water planets in the Sirius B system. They were quite capable of contacting us in the sea, although it was several thousand years before we advanced as a society. Their religious leaders, shall we call them, made sure they began working with us at an early stage, as it was understood that we would be bringing new blood to interact with these ancient societies.

What was their goal or purpose in contacting you?

It was simply to give a friendly hello, and they offered to work with us in the future, as they saw we were a benevolent society.

How many planets are you in contact with as a planetary society now?

Plenty — well over 200 at this time.

How long has your race been able to travel to other planets?

Millions of years.

That's the same for the stars?

That was a little different but not by too much. We experienced a rapid development in that area.

Was it because you were visited by other cultures?

Yes, they were ahead of us in development, so that greatly sped up our development too.

Was this well before you developed spaceships yourselves?

Oh, it was quite some time before we were able to construct our own. But our neighbors shared their information, so we made quick advances in space travel.

Were you provided with spaceships when you began to travel as a people?

Yes, but that was a stage a little further along, shall we say. First, our eventual friends came from the other planets in our star system. They came in peace and we were quite impressed with their advancement, as we were the "new kids on the block," I believe you would say. We came to the Sirius B system after almost all the others had been long established — and I mean *long* established.

When we developed to the point where we were, say, a couple of thousand years earlier than you are now, they began to visit and offer us any assistance in moving forward at a much faster rate. Naturally, we accepted their assistance, and that led to them picking up some of our representatives and taking them to the other planets in our star system to study and learn. This was — not counting some "joy rides" around the planet, as you might call them — our first foray into space.

As we grew in understanding and knowledge, eventually they taught us how to handle spacecraft, albeit small ones similar to the scout craft we have today. They loaned us these craft for our trips to nearby planets so they would not have to come and pick us up each time.

Is this common? Did they portal-hop (see glossary) or just travel at whatever normal speed the craft were capable of?

Already at that time, everyone had the knowledge of portal hopping, and the craft were capable of doing this. Unless we were taking some of our people on those joy rides around the planet, we used the portal hops ourselves.

From what I've heard of the Sirians, you have advanced over a period of millions of years without backtracking as has happened on Earth. Is that true?

Yes, mostly. We have had our wars and have backtracked, as you call it, or reversed our progress for a while, but overall we have consistently progressed in our scientific knowledge to a very advanced state compared to Earth. That said, since this will be read one day, your advancement in working with negative energy is far beyond what any other society we've found in the universe has been able to do. Now as you progress, your scientific achievements will come rapidly as you emerge from the third dimension to the fourth and fifth.

We will, of course, be there to assist you as much as we're allowed, but the barrier that has been present will one day soon be taken down so that you can get on with the next major phase of your development and bring small amounts of negativity to other planets in the universe. It is an exciting time for everyone, although there is consternation everywhere that we are about to have growing pains, as you term them.

At what level of the fifth focus do you operate on your planet?

Certainly we have operated or existed in the fifth focus for many hundreds of thousands of years, but our level — let's see if you can receive it today — is more on the level of a 5.4. Yes, that is fairly close. I know you thought it would be higher, but again we look at the reason we are waiting in great anticipation for contacts to begin with your society so that we can begin to grow again.

[Author's Note: Yes, folks, I'm really surprised at how low that number is, given the several-million-year head start the rest of the Federation has on us. I guess we have our work cut out for us to get things moving again to help everyone raise their vibrational levels!]

CHAPTER 6

STAR WARS

What was the planet with the largest population that you contacted and also the smallest?

From two sides of the spectrum. The largest one we have contacted personally is a planet in a far-off galaxy that had several million inhabitants. Earth is quite unique in how large a population it has compared to most of the planets in the universe.

And the smallest population?

Well, just a few hundred. They are beings who seem to be part of the landscape. Each of these beings requires a lot of space.

Were all these planets peaceful, or did they have any violence or wars?

A good question. They were all relatively peaceful. The ones we contacted do not have anywhere close to the violence you live with on Earth. That makes you unique too, you see.

If you had wars in your past, didn't they produce a negative energy similar to what we live with?

No, not in the same way. Yes, there were wars, and yes, they did produce a negative energy. But that was dissipated quite quickly, you see — or perhaps you do not. It's difficult to explain in the time we have. We could have one of those book-length discussions on how these past wars were resolved and how peace was brought about. Those wars happened millions of years ago in your time, and there are no remnants that are or were left over.

The Reptilian War

How large were the space battles they had?

Oh, quite large — thousands of ships, if you can imagine. We actually had our own Star Wars, similar to some of the depictions in your movies and literature. Naturally, they were written and produced by those souls who had been incarnated at that time.

Did everyone use stargates during that time?

Yes and no. Many gates were guarded so that if an enemy ship came through, it would be immediately attacked and repelled.

Was your Federation of planets formed before or after the Star Wars?

Good question. As you might have guessed, that happened after the Star Wars. It was put into motion so that we would all become neighbors and not enemies. It has worked superbly for us, you see.

What groups were fighting each other?

The reptilians fought against an amalgamation of other planets, including my own, and a number of others you would recognize but others you wouldn't. Now we are friends.

When the reptilians attacked, why did they pick you specifically, or did they actually include you with thousands of other planets? How large was this conflict?

It was quite large; we were just a part of the war. This was a huge conflict — far beyond even your science fiction writers. And yes, each side lost dozens of planets during this long conflict. But to answer your question, yes, we were just one part of it, but it was right at our doorstep, you would say. It wasn't something that was occurring halfway across the universe, although it certainly took on that aspect as we counterattacked.

Did they make any demands before attacking?

Yes, some demands, but they were told no. Still, you could compare it to your December 7 attack of Pearl Harbor. It was quite sudden and not completely unexpected, but yes, it was still a shock to the planets. The reptilians wished to take over certain planets, so they did with great loss of life for the inhabitants of those planets.

What resources did the reptilians want?

You name it. Many are so exotic you have not discovered their uses yet. As I mentioned before, we cannot tell you what these resources are. All we will be able to do is say, "Hang on to this resource in the future, as you'll need it." So I am not allowed to give you that information, according to the Earth Directive (see glossary).

Then did they suddenly appear in the Sirius B system one day, or were the first battles fought elsewhere?

We were given some warning that battles had begun — enough to quickly form guardian ships or assign them to portals.

Were there actually battles fought on the ground by the reptilians and the defenders of any particular planets?

Not in the sense or the same manner as depicted in your movies. Yes, there were ground troops, but much of the battles were fought in the air. When the air defenses were destroyed, then came the troops.

Would I recognize the star system that was first attacked?

No. You would have to have much greater knowledge of the star systems than you do now. It is a more remote one than normally discussed.

How close is the reptilian galaxy to the Milky Way?

Quite close, in actuality. You could say a hop, skip, and a jump away.

What was the goal of the reptilians when they started the Star Wars?

It was simple greed at that time. The reptilians decided they wished to have more worlds and more resources at their disposal, and instead of trading for the resources, they decided to just take what they wanted and do it by force. This is still played out on a much smaller scale on Earth, but back then it involved billions and billions of beings.

It quickly grew to mammoth proportions as far as the number of worlds that were involved, as the worlds being subjugated naturally resisted and asked for our — I'm using the collective here — assistance to rid their worlds of the reptilian forces. The Star Wars, as you call it, lasted for thousands of years, and there were many battles fought over these resources until the reptilians had enough and withdrew. Now the reptilians are kissing cousins, shall I say, and we are all at peace with each other. Everyone is allowed to travel wherever they wish. That's a very short version of the very lengthy story of a colossal war between worlds.

How long did the Star Wars last in Earth years?

Quite a long time. It was thousands of years in Earth time — yes, you are receiving me correctly. This wasn't just a puny war between a few planets — these were whole galaxies involved in the war. The depictions in some of your movies and TV series was somewhat accurate from the standpoint of huge forces and many, many war craft involved.

How were the planets able to repel the reptilians during the Star Wars?

Certainly the ships can produce great beams of energy that can destroy any ship known to exist. The idea of having a force field protection that your science-fiction movies show is quite accurate too. But one energy beam can be greater than another ship's ability to repel, so it is not always black and white; or to use another phrase, it's hard to compare apples and oranges, but you can compare large apples with small apples.

So once the shock of being attacked was over, great forces were melded together from many star systems to repel the attacks, and this eventually became the Federation. Then it was a matter of taking the fight to the reptilians' galaxy too. Again, this took thousands of universal years (see glossary). This was not something that was fought and was over in a short time. It dragged on and on.

Were there any planets or stars destroyed during that massive war?

Certainly there were a number destroyed — both planets and stars. After all, destroy a star and its planets are destroyed too. It was very nasty business back then.

That's something I never thought of. How many beings died during these Star Wars?

Literally billions, as we count beings that you might not recognize as being sentient but are. Your society still has the overall belief that animals are dumb, but they are not. So billions and billions of beings died.

How long did it take to become friends with the reptilians again after the war was over?

Quite a long time. Naturally, there was a healthy mistrust in whether the peace would hold, plus there was that same feeling of loss any being will have in the deaths of friends and family. It was very difficult, but we slowly returned to peaceful ways, and they did too. It was in all of our best interests to do so.

War Close to Earth

Are there one or more downed spaceships on the Moon?

Quite so. Certainly they cannot be seen by the naked eye from a satellite. The spaceship you previously discussed with your guardian angel does exist, and it was a casualty of the Star Wars when both ships emerged from portals quite close to each other. The reptilians immediately attacked and the ship had no chance, as its defenses were not activated in time. All lives were lost, as there are gaping holes in the hull from the weapons used on it. It was over quite quickly, you see.

I might add you will discover this ship one day, but as your angel mentioned before, it would be dangerous to explore this back side of your Moon until satellites are installed that can keep track of work there too. This will take many years, as you might imagine.

How many other spacecraft are there on the surface?

There are a small number, perhaps ten or so. The mothership, as you call it, was the largest.

Why was the ship and the reptilian craft even in this area, as we were not on the usual trade lanes, were we?

No, but keep in mind all those portals I said were here. They were on their way to other places in the universe and happened to cross paths at the wrong time. They were not fighting over Earth. It just happened to be a way station for transits. Millions of beings were lost in that war, but we do not dwell on that now. Peace is here between all beings — at least all members of the Federation and the reptilians.

Peace Negotiations

Was there one individual or a group that negotiated the peace?

Definitely, as in any large negotiation, there were many specialists in this type of agreement. It would be somewhat similar to negotiations that you've had on

Earth to end your wars. This was not at a point when one side was so defeated that the other could dictate terms.

This war could have lasted for thousands more years had there not been some agreement negotiated for it to end. Each side had their chief negotiators along with large staffs that worked on specific sections of the peace accord.

Would you know if I had a life during this wartime period?

Of course you did. A number of lives, as this went on for such a long time.

Did I take part in the peace process?

Not directly. You acted more from an advisory capacity, shall we say.

What do you mean by saying I was in an "advisory capacity" in the negotiations to end the war with the reptilians?

You were in more of a leadership capacity — somewhat on the spiritual side. Yes, you're receiving me correctly. You used your talents to suggest different things to bring to the negotiations from your lives on Earth that were quite helpful in making progress in these negotiations. That's among the many special gifts that you have attained — the ability to suggest the easiest path to agreement and reconciliation.

You said I had several lives during that period of history, but you also said I always acted as an advisor, not a participant or not seemingly in another job — ambassador, space crewman of any type, or any other of many hundreds of possibilities. Why did I incarnate into whatever religious order, priesthood, or whatever system you had over and over again?

I understand. It is because your soul resonates with that type of service, and you have had thousands of lives in which you served in that capacity. If you wanted to compare it to something on Earth, it would be like being the Dalai Lama in each life. It is not exactly the same as that, but this is a good analogy. You have been able to lead and suggest many things over the course of those lives and the ones since then that were of help to our people and even to many other planets in this Federation. I know it does not seem as if you could do such a thing while veiled in this life, but you have made many important contributions to not only your own people, but to many, many other beings in this universe. You did help bring an end to the Star Wars, although it did take you several lives to do this.

Antura, was the Earth Experiment already in operation or just in the planning stages during the time of the Star Wars?

Good question. Yes, it was underway although in a very early stage, shall we say.

Why was the Earth Experiment needed when so much negativity was released during the Star Wars?

Negativity was released, but because no one could handle it, this negativity was released or pushed aside. The purpose of the Earth Experiment was to learn how to handle negativity and work with it, as you have done. No other society in this universe has been able to work with it as you have now.

No other beings in the universe have karma or the need to balance that we do — is that correct?

Correct. No one else is veiled except Earth humans.

Does the reptilian race mostly inhabit one galaxy?

Yes, primarily, although they do have worlds they inhabit scattered across the universe. After all, Creator likes variety, and they are one of the varieties of life.

You said there are reptilian worlds in the Milky Way Galaxy. Were these there from the beginning, or were they planets they took over and refused to give up?

A little of both. As I mentioned before, Creator likes variety so, yes, there were a few planets with reptilians. And then, yes, there are a few planets they absorbed into the reptilian system.

What percentage of the universe is reptilian?

Much less than they think. Really 10 percent or less is the best answer. We're not exactly sure ourselves, as we are constantly exploring galaxies. There are millions of them, so you can imagine just exploring one galaxy can take thousands of years of your time.

Were there a variety of reptilians that fought in the Star Wars, or was there one major group?

No, there was a wide variety. My understanding is that no particular group participated more than the others.

Do the reptilians lay just one or two eggs, or do they lay bunches, say up to thirty or more?

Certainly it all depends on the species, but most lay a few eggs — not just one or two. And yes, some are capable of laying a number of eggs.

I would think that there are some events to celebrate, such as the end of the Star Wars?

Yes, you are correct. We do have a day of remembrance for those lost on both sides of the war.

What about a day to remember the forming of the Federation?

Yes, that too is celebrated, although in a more low-key way, shall we way.

CHAPTER 7

THE FEDERATION OF PLANETS

How many star systems does the Federation represent?

Let's see if you can receive these numbers. Yes, thirty-six is very close to the number.

Are there Federations in other galaxies?

Yes and no. It is just an amazingly different experience each time we venture out to another galaxy. Their makeup is sometimes so different that it is impossible to communicate, and we've been doing this, may I remind you, for several million years in Earth time.

You have stated that the purpose of the Federation is security and trade. Any other purpose?

Yes, naturally there is a constant exchange of ideas and scientific development. Trade is also important, because some planets are awash in certain elements that other planets have none of and vice versa, so there is a lively barter exchange of elements and, of course, goods. We are a pretty happy family of planets, although not without our own disagreements. Most of the time, everything runs smoothly.

Is there someone from one of the member planets who is appointed or perhaps elected to lead the Federation?

Yes, there is. It is more of a figurehead title, but this person or being, shall we say, works to bring everyone together and discuss our mutual problems.

Are all the members in the fifth focus?

Yes and no. They are all in the fifth focus, but certainly a number of them have the ability to be in the seventh focus too. It becomes much easier to move between focuses after you reach, say, a certain level of the fifth.

Antura, will any trading be established between Earth and the rest of the Federation after we have contact?

Very little at first, but certainly there will be some things we will be able to trade with you. We will not be allowed to sell or barter devices, because that would preclude you from inventing them yourselves. We would not want to deprive your planet of any of its resources, as much of these resources will be needed in the coming years. This includes resources you do not know you have and resources you have not yet figured out how to use in new ways. Again, this is all part of your progress. We may not even be allowed to point out the resources to you, but perhaps we can reveal a little at a time. We might be allowed to say, "You will find 'this' to be an important resource in the future, so be sure to take care of it."

Is it your understanding that the Federation and, more particularly, the beings from the Sirius star system are the protectors of Earth and this experiment?

Yes, that is correct. We are your friendly protectors, as we have been for many millions of years. We all wanted this Earth Experiment to succeed, you see, and now it finally has, although it may not appear that way to you yet. But we are the equivalent of your long-lost relatives, as you and the rest of Earth will learn over the coming years.

So what did we need protection from?

Oh, that would be a long list. Naturally, there were even conflicts between us and other worlds that are now part of this Federation. Plus, the most danger to you came from outside influences who have not contributed any part of your DNA that make up the Earth human today. These beings had to be kept at a distance in order for this experiment to survive and thrive per Creator's wishes. Remember that we work at Creator's behest. Creator wanted this experiment to take place and felt that it would be successful. Creator was questioned by other creators who either weren't sure or completely doubted that it would ever be a success.

Are there negative or malevolent ETs on Earth's surface or below it?

No, not now. Again, the Federation Directive has established a zone around your planet that cannot be breached. The beings trying to breach this zone would find themselves in serious trouble with the whole Federation. Those on the surface may live among you as part of their studies, or they may live underground, but those interests are purely to study and do not interact in a negative or violent way.

Is there a common language or written language used for Federation affairs, or is that not needed?

It's really not needed, as we have all these translation devices that are so far advanced they can translate the smallest meaning of a given language or writing. There can be no hidden agendas, shall we call them, of a society trying to twist something around to its own benefit. These nuances are instantly recognizable and therefore are not even attempted.

When you greet other Federation members, is there a universal greeting such as our old TV show Star Trek *had?*

No, but we did find that amusing. We adopt the greeting of each being, and our greeting is more of a mental greeting than any set of physical gestures. We basically wish them long lives — something to that effect. It varies somewhat, but yes, "good life" is one of the greetings.

Is there a world either in the Federation or outside of it that has a race of beings similar to the Vulcans in the Star Trek *series and movies?*

Yes, of course there is. They were created in your stories to represent those who are already in existence elsewhere. That's part of the lure of these sci-fi movies and TV shows for you. You will feel right at home when you see and visit the worlds depicted in your science fiction. Again, as you know, these stories are written by people who have experienced lives in which they met creatures and beings from all over the universe.

Are the Federation meetings held in halls, or are they just done by tuning in from all over?

Yes, much more the latter. We have no need for gathering. You have video conferencing now. We just have a much more advanced version of this in which it seems we are gathered next to the person or being speaking. We are able to tune into their feelings so that we can understand the nuances of what they are communicating.

Antura, there are not any major conflicts going on in the universe at the present time are there?

No. Surely there might be some local conflicts when two planets have disagreements, but there are none in our Federation nor any of the other galaxies that I know about. One of the functions of the Federation is to arbitrate, if you will. But what I think you're asking is if there are any major wars, and there are none that we are aware of. There are only small localized conflicts in which we or some other federation steps in "so cooler heads can prevail," to use your expression.

Have any of your spaceships been caught in the explosions of planets or stars, or do you have sufficient knowledge of these things to be able to avoid such catastrophes?

Yes, this happened much more in the earlier days of exploration — and I'm talking about the Federation as a whole here, with our planet included. Now, we have developed our technology to such a degree that we can tell well in advance if a star or planet is ready to explode, and we stay a safe distance away. But to answer your question fully, yes, this did happen in the past — with great loss of life. That was part of our space exploration.

Antura, do any of the Federation planets have copies of, say, the library of Alexandria?

No. There is no need, as we have much better ways to keep records of all of your time periods than to rely on this ancient library. As has been discussed with you before, time is an illusion to you; and we have the ability to travel back in time, should we desire to do so, and explore any part of your history we wish to.

Federation Membership

How many of the planets in the universe are you aware of that have humanoids?

Good question again — probably on the order of over 50 percent. That's a best guess right now, we'll say.

Okay. Why are there so few planets in the Federation? It would seem to me that it should be much larger if you've had millions of years.

Yes, it would seem that way on the surface, but in actuality, this group of planets have many things in common between them. Our interests are basically the same, as compared to other planets perhaps. We are also geographically close to each other, and this helps foster trade and the exchange of ideas.

It can also act as protection if any threat develops to our security and ability to live life in a peaceful manner, as was the case in the past but is not now at the present. Obviously, over millions of years, you will have conflicts, so you'll someday see maps of the locations of these planets, as they are in the same quadrant of the galaxy, shall we say.

Are these planets just in the Milky Way Galaxy, as we call it?

Yes, you're correct in that supposition.

If Sirius B is approximately 440 light-years away from us, what are the closest and most distant Federation star systems?

Not a lot closer — certainly the Pleiades you are thinking of is close. There is one a little closer. And the farthest away — well, it is over 300 light-years from you; I'll say that for now.

Antura, I think I got in the way again on the light-year distances of the Pleiades star system and others. Is it true that the Pleiades is 500 light-years away from us?

Yes, that's correct. The Pleiades is 500 or so light-years away. Yes, you had a little difficulty with those numbers, and I knew that you would read and return, so I did not wish to upset our communications by saying no, you're not correct. It would have affected the other questions you were asking.

Okay, so if the Pleiades is 500 light-years away, are there any other Federation members farther away than that?

Oh yes, quite a few in fact. You'll find them at even double the distance of the Pleiades. With interstellar travel, what seems a long way is not. As it was explained to you before, though there are limits to the distances one can travel through stargates, hopping from one to another can take you across the universe. It just takes a little time to go that far, as you can imagine. It's similar to those Southwest Airlines flights you have taken during which you land in one city, are there for only fifteen or twenty minutes, and off you go again. Yes, I know all about them and of course all about you. That's part of my studies on your planet. We amass a great deal of information about a planet before contact, but in your case, it's actually double and triple what we would accumulate for any other planet. As I have said before, your planet is unique in all the universe.

Is Arcturus — the planet anyway — a member of the Federation and are they thirty-seven light-years away from us too?

Yes, on all counts. Several planets in their star system are members, and yes, the distance away is approximately thirty-seven light-years.

Antura, is everyone in the Federation so advanced that there are no illnesses? And do people transition easily at the end of their natural lives?

Yes to both questions. Illnesses are extremely rare and are easily handled and corrected. Only in the Earth Experiment are there illnesses. But keep in mind that we have millions of years of development, so any DNA strand or gene that is off kilter is easily fixed. We do contact some planets where the inhabitants are not as far advanced as, say, Earth. They might have some local diseases they have not known how to eradicate, but we allow them to correct these on their own.

We do easily transition at the end of our lives on all Federation planets. Life as we have discussed is much easier, which is why on my planet, for example, we typically live 1,200 to 1,500 years. And that's why on Earth you do not, because your lives are so difficult. After you have been in the fifth focus for a little while, you will see your lives stretch out, as your lives will become so much easier and less stressful because you will find cures for all known diseases.

But your spiritual evolution is at a plateau? You have evolved there as far as you can?

Yes, in a way. We have reached a plateau, but when Earth humans come knocking on our doors, we will see more evolvement. Your society will be a catalyst.

How many planets are you in contact with as a planetary society now?

Plenty — well over 200 at this time.

How many planets are you aware of in the universe that are inhabited by intelligent beings?

We are aware of many thousands. Some wish to be left strictly by themselves.

Am I correct in saying that the Sirian planets make up about one-fourth of the Federation planets?

Yes, that's about right. Perhaps a little higher percentage but not much.

So the Pleiadians make up what percentage?

A little less than we have in numbers, but they make up for it in variety, you see.

How many of the planets in the Federation have two or more intelligent forms of life that take part in the Federation affairs?

Certainly more than half. Some even have multiples as you suggested. On my planet, both the land dwellers and the amphibians both take part in Federation affairs. Keep in mind that for the most part, we are a very happy, content group of worlds, so there are certainly challenges to work through, but these are small in comparison to what you have to deal with.

Are any of these life forms insect in nature?

Yes, of course. There are quite a few planets inhabited by insect-type creatures that are members of the Federation.

No reptilians are members, are they?

No, they tend to keep to themselves.

How many of the worlds have humanoids?

Quite a few again. Certainly over one-third.

How many Federation worlds have amphibians like you?

Not as many — less than 10 percent.

How many worlds have what we consider fish that would be intelligent?

Oh, quite a few — more than 20 to 30 percent.

What other types of life on Federation planets have I not covered?

There is intelligent life connected with the plant world. Animals that you call by name definitely have a presence on many of the worlds.

Explorations

Is there another federation of planets, or are there several federations that you are good friends with?

Yes, several, spread across the universe — actually many more than that. Some are smaller and some larger in the number of planets they represent.

So you have good relationships with all these federations?

Yes, some better than others. Some are more formal than others, as you cannot imagine on your third-dimensional level the great differences there are out there across the universe. Some wish to be left strictly alone to their own pursuits, and we honor those requests.

Do you have an ambassador on each Federation planet?

No, that is not needed with our instant communication. We can instantly be in touch with another world or planet, so there is no need for someone to be physically there, although representatives of all the planets do get together occasionally.

Then since the Federation has only a couple of hundred planets that are members, how many other federation-type groups are there in the Milky Way Galaxy, as we call it?

A dozen or so. Not too many when you think of how many suns and planets there are, but you will find there are reasons for the lack of groups. There is a huge difference in how far developed these planets are, and some groups of planets do not desire to have this type of mutual relationship.

Are there federations larger than yours?

Quite so. Some comprise up to 1,000 planets. And to answer the next question, yes, we have relationships with all of them — very cordial ones, I might add, with perhaps one exception. That federation just wishes to keep to itself.

Over the millions of years the Federation of Planets has been exploring the universe, what percentage of it have you been able to explore?

A fairly large percentage. Somewhere around the 70 percent level, perhaps more. After all, even though there are millions of stars, we don't need to visit every one of them, as some — actually a fairly sizable number — are devoid of intelligent life. The planets are in stages of development that will take thousands to millions of years to develop to, say, your stage. Our instruments are quite sensitive and quickly give us readings on these stars to know whether to explore them further or not. Along with that, we have people who have the ability to see things without instruments. Dozens of stars can be read and deleted if no intelligent life is detected.

It's hard for me to believe you said that the Federation has explored about 70 percent or more of the universe?

That's correct, and I understand the reason for the question. Yes, it has been explored over millions of years in universal time.

More than 10 billion years?

Yes, we are talking ancient. Certainly it would have to take that amount of time when you consider how many galaxies there are in the universe. It's a huge number, and each year we still have motherships and scout ships going out to far-flung galaxies to explore and check for life in them. Obviously, most are teeming with life, so it certainly can take years just to explore one galaxy. Look how fast you are progressing. By the year 3250 or so, you will be able to travel to other star systems yourselves. It did not happen that fast with our Federation planets. When you triple or quadruple that time frame, you will see the time it took for us to be able to learn how to move from star to star.

Your planet has known other intelligent human developments, but they are not written about in your current history nor are they readily available to you memory-wise, since you're veiled. We are not veiled, so it is easy for us to access our past lives and build on those. But none of us has been able to do what you have done, as has been discussed many times in the past — and that's your ability to exist in a highly negative environment. So this will be what you bring to the Federation table, shall we call it, and you will be the catalyst for our further growth.

Antura, when the Federation explores a new galaxy, does it send one spacecraft or mothership, or does it send ten, a hundred, or how many?

Good question. Yes, typically at least two or three motherships, as you call them, will be assigned to explore a galaxy never explored before. As you know, we portal-hop, as you call it, and we can move quickly across the universe to any faraway galaxy. And certainly the reverse is true too. After a few universal years — let's say perhaps one hundred for purposes of discussion — the mothership will return and a new crew will take the place of the old one and continue the work, switching off every so often until the galaxy has been explored and those planets with sentient beings have been contacted and studied.

It can be very discreet or very open, depending upon the situation. Sometimes we are not welcomed at all, and we honor requests to leave and have no more contact with that planet or solar system. It varies greatly, as you can imagine. But we have personnel who are experts in first contact and can pretty easily tell when we will be welcome and when we won't.

As you can imagine, however, this can be a very arduous and detailed job of exploration, so it may take many universal years before the work is completed on a whole galaxy. Just look at how large the Milky Way Galaxy is, and then multiply that by a few billion times.

Scientists estimate there are 17 billion Earth-size planets in our Milky Way galaxy. What is the actual number?

Definitely much more than that. Try one trillion on for size.

Yet you say that your Federation only has 200 planets as members.

Yes, it seems a tiny fraction, but keep in mind the enormous differences between planets and their level of development. Plus, keep in mind I did mention there are other federations or groupings of planets.

Earth and the Federation

Are we already members of the Federation?

Not yet. That is misinformation being put out. You will not become official members for some time, as we want you to understand what the Federation is and what it does. I'm speaking of the general public, as naturally there are those in government who know a lot more than they are releasing to the public. So in due course, you will wish to be a member, first by voting on it in the United Nations and then affirming it in each country.

What will we be able to contribute to the Federation?

Ah, you have much to contribute. As I mentioned before, your Explorer Race has made great progress in an area that everyone else has failed at — working with negativity. And though that sounds simple to you, I can assure you it is not, my friend. You will introduce games and small amounts of negativity, as you have already been told that will cause all of the societies you encounter to begin growth again. You will be the catalysts of the universe.

Are you saying that really the only thing we have to offer the Federation is our ability to work with negativity?

In a way, yes. It's hard to understand on the level you're at now what a major accomplishment this is. You're truly the only planet that's ever been able to do this. So we might have our great inventions and all, but the one thing we have not been able to do is what you're doing on a daily basis on your planet — working with this energy in massive amounts. You will teach us how to do this too.

How many ships are currently monitoring Earth from space? I saw that someone claimed there are thousands.

No, there are not thousands. There are a lot fewer than 100 but, at times, as many as fifty or sixty, depending on who is coming and going as they finish their studies and move on. The Federation carefully monitors these ships, especially the ones from outside the galaxy and even outside this universe, to make sure they keep within the bounds of the Earth Directive, which lays out what they can and cannot do at this time. Naturally, this will change and evolve as you bridge over to the fifth focus, but there is a pretty tight rein, we'll call it, over activities around Earth at the present time.

Other Planetary Relationships

Are the Zetas members of the Federation? And isn't the Zeta Reticuli system 39½ light-years distant?

Yes, they are now members. We have very good relations with them now, although that was not always the case in the past. Yes, it did have to do with them at a younger stage interfering with you, although we understood their need to do so. We contacted their earlier selves to assist in fixing their birthrate problem.

At one point, they were on their own, to put it nicely. We had many talks and negotiations and such with them, and we were successful in pointing them in the right direction. They were able to save themselves by creating the Earth-Gray hybrid that was at one time on your timeline but now is not. You will not need to spend future lives there, unless a specific soul or group of souls wishes to do so.

But I assume we will meet these hybrids in the future?

Oh yes, quite so. After all, they have your DNA mixed in with theirs now, which makes for a unique being.

Do you work with a planet called Nibiru?

Yes, to a certain extent. No, they are not members of the Federation.

Why wouldn't they be?

That is a good question. Yes, they do claim Federation membership, but that is not quite accurate. It is complicated, but they are not full members. We do work with them, as their planet has an unusual orbit, and yes it does look like a comet if seen in the sky.

They claim to be our forefathers 262,000 years ago.

Yes, they do have a connection with you but not what they claim — that they were your forefathers per se.

Where are they located?

Quite far from you at the present time. They have been asked not to interfere with you at this time.

So am I receiving this information correctly, Antura, or have I allowed my normal skepticism to interfere?

No, you are receiving this information correctly. The Nibiru planet is not a member of the Federation at this time.

Antura, why are we expected to become a member of the Federation of Planets even though you said Nibiru is just associated with the Federation?

Theirs is a special situation in which they went against the Directive by interfering with the Earth Experiment, although certainly they were involved too at one time. You could call it probation in your words.

Antura, is there sexual diversity on your planet? And I'll also ask is there a norm on the Federation planets?

Yes, there is some sexual diversity in my society, and we honor those decisions. Regarding the other Federation planets, they are quite diverse, as there are people who are male and female at the same time who can conceive and have children. There are heterosexual people and beings, there are those who lay eggs, and there are the insect types who have all sorts of different reproductive systems. You can imagine that the study of sexuality in the Federation could take years. It is a very complex subject due to the very nature of the diversity of the beings who live on and in these 200-member planets. So almost anything you can imagine or not imagine would fall into categories.

How many species in the Federation contributed souls as compared to DNA?

Naturally, all 200 planets have, plus planets not in the Federation such as the reptilians; but yes, others contributed to the Earth Experiment. It was not limited to just our group, but a number of other species who the Creator thought would be a good mix for you in this experiment.

Antura, you said a little over 50 percent of the souls on your planet have had Earth lives. So would that percentage be about the same for other Federation planets?

No. Certainly each of the Federation planets have souls having Earth lives, but the percentage varies greatly from a low of, say, less than 10 percent to a high of over 70 percent.

Would the high percentage be more from, say, the Pleiadians?

Yes, exactly. They, along with the Arcturians and Sirians, have the highest percentage of participants.

Are all the planets in the Pleiades members of the Federation?

Yes. They do have a number of planets, but all are members.

What percentage are humanoid, Antura?

Definitely over 50 percent.

Does it go as high as 75 percent?

Yes, overall they are mostly humanoid but do have variety, as again, most planets do.

How many planets are there in the Pleiades, Antura, that are members of the Federation — over twenty, let's say?

Yes. Again their numbers would be similar to our Sirius B system — in the mid-twenties. It might seem that they should have many more, but these are the planets that have intelligent life on them. Please keep in mind that even in our star systems, there are various stages of development that have been around for billions of years. I will refer to our own example in which we settled on our water planet some 18 million years ago, yet there were already societies much older than that in existence in the system for well over one billion years. It is like that all over the universe.

Is there one planet in the Federation that you work with more than any other planet?

No, perhaps one group of planets would be a closer answer. Naturally, we would tend to work with those in our own solar system more than others due to their close location or presence. Those relationships date back many millions of years, so there is the comfort factor.

Is there something important about Orion's Belt?

There are Federation planets there, so certain people will have originated there — not to the same large extent as the Sirians, Arcturians, and Pleiadians — but they did contribute to you in the past.

Antura, astronomers say our galaxy alone has billions of stars and now billions, if not trillions, of planets. Is it your knowledge that every sun in our galaxy has one or more planets circling it, or is that too general?

Perhaps that is a little general, as there are some lonely stars out there with no planet companions yet, but they are mostly new stars. You will find as you travel out to the stars yourself that almost every one of them will seem to have a plethora of planets attached to them.

The Earth Directive

Did the Earth Directive come into being before or after the sinking of Atlantis?

It came or was created just before the sinking, as all of our instruments pointed out that the continent would sink.

Who created or was responsible for the Earth Directive?

The whole Federation had a meeting, and the Directive came out of that meeting. It basically said we were not to interfere with your progress and the Earth Experiment. This was also in consultation with the Creator, you see, not just a bunch or group of beings from different worlds trying to clean up the mess they had made, albeit with good intentions. Therefore, we have remained unobtrusive, shall we say, for the past few thousand years, and were really not sure if you would destroy yourselves until you passed that magic date that Master Kryon has mentioned before. The planetary members of the Federation were ecstatic; I can assure you.

Which planet proposed the Earth Directive?

One of the members of the Federation but really more of a council, you would call it. It was then quickly written, shall we say, and put into effect.

Could you explain in more detail for those reading this book the Federation's Directive regarding Earth and when it was implemented?

Yes. It basically states that none of the Federation planetary societies are to interfere in any way with the Earth population, other than in noninvasive ways such as manipulating your etheric bodies during sleep time and even then only with the souls' permission. It specifically states no kidnapping, physical body studies, and so on. It further states that the Federation planets cannot give any person on this planet information unless it is cleared with your Earth advisors, we will call them. When in doubt — hands off.

This directive was agreed to about twenty years ago, give or take a year. It took a little more time to implement it. Naturally, its purpose was and is to take the fear out of being abducted, as it was known then that you would soon be having public contact and it was not good to scare the population. Plus, the Creator wants you to reinvent the wheel, shall we call it, as It believes you will find better ways of doing things.

Can you give me more information about what's contained in the Earth Directive — sort of one, two, three?

Yes, I'll try.

1. There shall be no more abductions of Earth people for any experiments.
2. There shall be no assistance given regarding inventions without Federation approval.
3. Contact with Earth people and their governments will only be made with Federation approval.
4. Contact with governmental leaders will be limited to fostering an understanding that we wish no harm, and contact will not, under any circumstances, include providing them with any devices that they can use to their benefit or to the detriment of another country or people.
5. There is to be a continuing series of flyovers to remind people of our presence as well as for photographic purposes when we know there are photographers recording the event.
6. Studies can continue to be made and readings taken from our spacecraft but not of people taken into the spacecraft.
7. No spacecraft from outside this Federation will be allowed to interfere with the Earth Experiment. They will only be allowed to take readings as our Federation ships do. Any attempts to interfere will be met with force.

That should give you some idea of the restrictions set up in the Earth Directive to protect you.

I seem to be confused about the Earth Directive. You said the Earth Directive was originally created at the time of Atlantis, and then another time you said it was created twenty years ago to stop the abductions and interference. It seems, perhaps, you inferred the same regarding the Nibiruans. Please clear this up for me.

Yes, the original Earth Directive was not called that specifically at that time. It was originally just a warning to stay away from you when it was obvious that the islands of Atlantis were going to sink into the ocean. So to answer your question: The Earth Directive came about by combining all the rules, which had slowly come into effect over a long period of time. It was felt that there needed to be more specific guidance about what societies could and could not do. Up to that time, there was sort of a hodgepodge of rules and even suggestions, nothing formal. This clarified everything, but not until approximately twenty years ago were these finalized.

Why didn't our ET protectors protect the Earth people against the intrusions and kidnappings.

Again, this was one of those rules clarified after the horse had gotten out of the barn, to use one of your old sayings. It was not a problem before the Zetas began kidnapping and using earthlings to create their hybrid race, as they were dying out.

Also keep universal time in mind. What was twenty years to you was only a couple of years in universal time. I can assure you this was handled as fast as possible, given the fact that everyone had to agree to these rules.

CHAPTER 8

TIMELINES

Before I begin with my questions to Antura, I need to explain what timelines are. Otherwise, you'll feel as if you walked into a middle of the conversation.

My guardian angel says that each soul fragment has twelve parallel, or simultaneous, lives on Earth. He calls it the twelve timelines. There are twelve "yous" who were born on different frequencies. Just imagine twelve matrices.

The timelines are divided into fours and then subdivided into twos, with the lower timelines at lower frequencies as compared to the upper timelines. Therefore, timelines one through four, five through eight, and nine through twelve are grouped together with smaller changes in frequency but with a fairly large jump between four and five and eight and nine. Timeline twelve is nonphysical and is considered the perfect life by our souls. All others are compared with timeline twelve. Then the timelines are subdivided again, with one and two, three and four, five and six, seven and eight, nine and ten, and eleven and twelve closer in frequency to each other.

We are on timeline six — basically in the middle frequency — so there are versions of ourselves having harder lives living at lower frequencies, and the versions above are having easier lives at higher frequencies.

I'm sure this is confusing when you first read this information, so let me give you my personal example: On timelines one through eight, I attended Texas Christian University and received a Bachelor of Business Administration in finance. On timelines nine and above, I majored in English and became a science-fiction writer, later writing spiritual books.

On timelines one to eight, I went through the ROTC officers program in order to pay for my schooling and spent two years in the Army. On the upper timelines, I did not participate in ROTC, as there was no Vietnam War. They settled their differences with little conflict.

On the upper timelines, I married my college sweetheart, we moved to Colorado, we divorced, and I remarried and had children. On the lower timelines, my college sweetheart sent me a "Dear John" letter while I was in South Korea and she married someone else.

On timelines one to eight, I married my wife of today, but on the lower four of those timelines, we divorced eighteen years ago and both remarried. I'm still married to my wife on timelines five through eight.

Thirty years ago, my wife and I sold our international tour business and I started an international film and TV program distribution company, but on the lower timelines, I remained in the tour business. In 2005, I experienced congestive heart failure. It was caught just in time on these timelines, but I died on timelines one and two.

Figure 1 should give you at least a basic idea of how different our lives can be depending on which timeline we're on.

Antura, are you in touch with me on the other timelines?

Quite so. I do have different conversations, and to answer your next question: Yes, I started some time ago with the higher timelines.

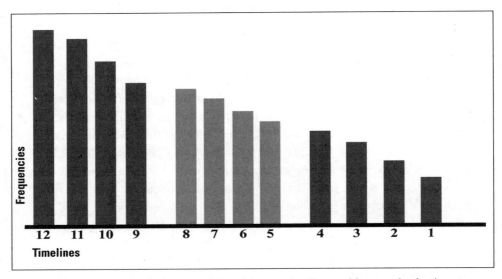

Figure 1: A simple chart displaying the relations between timelines and frequencies for the purpose of this discussion.

Are you in contact with all the higher timelines?

Yes, virtually all.

What about lower timelines — have you started with five yet?

Yes, that portion of you is just a little behind but not too much.

＊　　＊　　＊

I didn't catch you in the middle of something else did I, Antura?

No, our buddy — your guardian angel — kept me informed that you would awake on time today, so I was quite prepared.

Speaking of being prepared, aren't timelines five, seven, and eight, all meditating at the same time of day?

Yes, but again, I'm easily able to adapt to multiple questions coming in, as I am able to react and send these thought packets much faster than you can type. I also have the ability to carry on multiple conversations at the same time due to experience in this area. There is also another reason — your frequencies occur at different times for me, so I don't normally have all four happening at exactly the same time. That may be confusing, but different frequencies react differently in your time loop.[2]

So you have two reasons. First, that I can carry on multiple conversations if I must. Secondly and more intriguingly, being on a different frequency shifts you in universal time.

Is this common in the universe, having multiple timelines?

Oh no. This is unique for your planet and the Explorer Race in order to have as many experiences in one incarnation as possible. Quite unique!

Were you required to report to anyone each time you established a new contact with a different timeline here on Earth?

Certainly I did put this in my report, for both the council and all our citizens. Earth is a "hot topic," to use your phrase. As difficult as it is to get through to the third dimension — and add to that the fact you're veiled — when we make such a contact, it's news.

When you come, I guess you are just able to adjust the frequency a little in order to move between timelines.

Yes, quite so. They are minor changes, but they are significant for you.

Why is our future "fluid and forming" as you described before? Wouldn't it always have been that way?

No. The future was on one track, shall we say, and continued on that track for many millennia. Recently, though, that track has changed, and you are in unknown territory — territory never achieved before in Earth's history.

This is so fluid that it will not settle down for some time; I am using Earth

---

2 "Time loop" refers to a space-time continuum set up for the Earth Experiment so that souls can have lives simultaneously in the past, present, and future.

terms here. It will settle eventually, but if we go into the future, there are many probabilities. Although some are much more probable than others, it does not mean that a less-probable future might not happen.

That was the case in your 2008 presidential elections. The great probability was that Mrs. Clinton would become the next President. But your whole country, as has been described before for you, jumped almost to another higher timeline, amazing many of us. You have many challenges before you, and we are sitting in the stands, shall we say, waiting to see how you overcome them.

Antura, will you visit all the Earth's timelines or just five to eleven or twelve?

Good question. I will visit all the timelines, as there are those two people I mentioned before — one in our soul cluster — who are still leading lives in the lower timelines. Although they struggle to receive communications due to their lower vibrational rate, they do their work on these lower timelines too. I realize that you have been told that you have passed over in timelines one and two due to congestive heart failure, and that's true. On the other two timelines, you are not or have not been inspired to try the Gentle Way, and we may even do something with you there — or perhaps not, depending on the overall advancement of those timelines vibrationally.

I would like to travel to all the timelines to be able to describe to my readers — assuming I am still doing this at that time — the differences that I can see and feel.

Yes, we will consider that request.

What would you say is the basic difference between communicating with timelines seven and eight and timelines five and six?

I would say it is the ease in communication. Because you are at lower settings on timelines five and six — lower vibrationally, shall we say — it is much more difficult for you to accurately communicate with us. Even though timelines seven and eight are at a higher vibrational level, you are all still on a third-dimensional focus, but ease of communication certainly has to be your answer.

Antura, is there no need to communicate with timeline twelve since it's nonphysical?

Actually, I do briefly, but because it is a nonphysical timeline, what we do with that one is also nonphysical. I can quite easily download ideas, concepts, and so on.

How strange it is to learn about all these different timelines and lives?

It may seem a little confusing, and it certainly can be for us, even though we have experience in working with all timelines. It just makes our job that much more complex — not *too* difficult and complex, though, as each timeline is different. They are just a little different when they are connected together, but when they are separated, yes, it makes for a lot of record keeping, as you would term it.

How will I get the word out on timelines nine through eleven — video, books, or what — since I'm not in the film distribution business there?

Yes, both books and videos. Even though you don't have the focus there or the experience you have with video on these middle timelines, things are much easier to accomplish on the upper timelines and it is easier to disseminate information. You don't have the resistance there that you have here on the middle and lower timelines.

I assume you need to monitor all the timelines from five to eleven?

Quite so. Naturally it becomes easier with the higher timelines, as they are at higher vibrational levels due to their frequencies. I know we must struggle at times, but it is becoming easier and easier each time we communicate.

Then you know when each of the timelines will ask to visit in advance.

Quite so. I am informed of that by your own guardian angel. Keep in mind that he has been and will be my guardian angel too during my sojourns on Earth, so we have a pretty good rapport.

Time Loop

How is it that you cannot travel to your past — meaning all the rest of the universe, but ships from your past can materialize in our time loop?

Yes, that's an extremely complex question. You were also wondering how far out this time loop goes. There is a limit to its effects, but that is, in a way, how your spaceships will come from different timelines to visit us. We are not caught up in the time loop but must enter this time loop each time we travel to your solar system.

Antura, how many universal years will it be before an Earth starship visits your planet?

Surely you can imagine it will be quite some time. In your years, as I have said before, it will be around the 3250 era; but for us, it will only be a few hundred. Humans will still be alive here on your planet when we have our first callers from Earth, and yes, they will be from the upper timelines. Quickly thereafter, the others will follow. It seems confusing to you, but we understand the Earth Experiment and the difference in timelines, so we will know from which timeline the individual spaceships arrive.

When our timeline 6 spaceships go out to the stars, will they encounter other Earth spaceships from the other timelines?

A very interesting question. No, actually, they will not, although it will seem as if they are. It's as if they are in their own mini–force field or timeline. This is extremely difficult to explain on a third-dimensional basis, but you remain on your timeline, even after leaving Earth's space. I have told you in the past that we enter and then leave your time loop, but you do not. You exist at a certain frequency; therefore, you remain at that frequency in your travels to the stars.

CHAPTER 9

DISCLOSURE
IN 2013

I will take this time to ask if the European government will open the door, shall we say, to their secret files, and is that still scheduled for some time in 2013? If so, in what month?

Here you get into one of perhaps your least favorite subjects of probabilities, as it does have to do with humans and potentials. However, at the present, it is still dialed in for later in the summer or fall of 2013, depending on certain events beyond their control.

Will the first release of information about contacts with ETs be with a Western or Eastern European country?

Eastern, as you might have guessed. I know until recently you thought it would be Western, and I could not tell you differently until you asked.

So my guess is that it will be Russia?

There you have it. They are open — much more so than other countries. Therefore, the contact will be there.

Then are the Russian leaders making any preparations for the visit yet?

Only that they are slowly coming to realize that they can release the information about their contacts with ETs over many years and not cause panic in the streets.

Will other governments come forward in 2013 to release their secret material on contact, or will it be just one?

Oh, there will be a couple more, but the majority will hold off to see what the reaction of the general public will be.

What will be the flash point that will cause the European country to disclose?

Certainly I can't talk about what actual event will cause the leaders to open their secret archives on this, but there will be a slow but sure movement in that direction. If you pay attention to news stories and such, you will see it moving in that direction. We — meaning the Federation — will continue to have our ships seen on a regular basis to a point where we cannot be dismissed as weather balloons and other such nonsense.

What about Dmitry Medvedev — the Russian Prime Minister who let it slip in a conversation with Russian journalists that there are files? Will he be the one to release the information in 2013?

He will be part of the group of Russian leaders that decides the timing and whether the Russian people can handle the truth. That's the reason for the "trial balloons," as I believe you call them, with seemingly accidental information being given to reporters as if they thought the microphones were off. They wanted to see if there was any hysteria. Instead, there was just a lot of curiosity and desire for more information. The Russian people are quite used to secrets being slowly released by their KGB, so this will not have the same impact, shall we say, as if the CIA or some other governmental U.S.A. body released the same information on contacts.

Benefits of Disclosure

Antura, will there be any internal benefit to the people of Russia in being the first contact in public?

Most assuredly, there will be a wide range of emotions, including pride at being first. On the other end of the spectrum will be fear of space aliens taking over the planet. But overall, it will cause Russia to move much more quickly toward a more benevolent form of government, as they will wish to be recognized for their accomplishments and efforts. They will wish to be seen as leaders internationally, knowing they want to take advantage of being the first country contacted.

Will other governments come forward in 2013 to release their secret material on contacts, or will it be just one?

There will be a couple more, but the majority will hold off to see what the reaction of the general public is.

What is the highest probability that another country will release its information after the Russians?

For those who know about these contacts, it will take several months to see what reaction their own country has. It will take disclosures from one or two more Eastern Bloc countries before even the Western European countries will finally admit to these meetings, as they will be hounded by reporters from newspapers, magazines, and TV. That's why the first public contact will not occur until 2015, as more countries will need to release their secret files.

Will the United States Disclose?

Is it true that people in the United States government are now in favor of informing the public and or government about ETs?

There has been some movement there, thanks to your Mr. Obama taking office. Still, there is great concern and even fear of what revealing our presence will do to average people in America, whose belief systems would be turned upside down in many cases. We even recognize that there will be many people who will refuse to believe that there are ETs and will claim it is some sort of hoax. It will be too much for them to absorb initially and will take great time and patience to erase the mind programming to which they were subjected for over fifty years.

Then will the United States be one of these countries that will disclose in the months afterward?

Actually, no. There will be heated conversations about doing so — at least this is the highest probability at this time — but no decision will be made until they are forced to by the appearance of the Pleiadians.

CHAPTER 10

PLEIADIAN CONTACT IN 2015

Have the Pleiadians and the Sirians narrowed down the time frame for visitations in 2015 and 2017 yet?

Definitely. It will be the summer months in the Northern Hemisphere, as that is considered the ideal time — more on the order of July or August, you see.

Do any of the pyramids in Russia have anything to do with the contact in 2015?

Actually, no. That's a nice guess, but whether a particular country has pyramids or not does not have anything to do with us contacting them.

Are there any governments aware that the Pleiadians are coming in 2015?

Yes, several. They are quite nervous about this, as naturally much will come out about their prior meetings with the aliens, and some heads will roll because of this. Some would prefer that this never happens, but it will. Things will accelerate as that time approaches.

How large a spacecraft will be used by the Pleiadians for the first contact?

Definitely not the size of a mothership, more on the order of a medium-sized scout craft. It will be large enough to make everyone sit up and take notice but not so large as to scare people, more on the order of forty to fifty feet in diameter.

Will the Pleiadians use translator devices, or will they speak multiple languages?

They will use translator devices.

When they use these devices, will they choose a tonal quality that is pleasing to the person they are speaking to?

Quite so. It will also reflect that being's essence, shall we call it, so that the language used will sound exactly like someone would sound if he or she speaks the language. Again, these are extremely sophisticated devices, and they are able to handle every nuance of a language so that it sounds completely natural to the beings they are speaking to.

When the Pleiadians make first contact, will the press be screened to make sure no one will have heart attacks or strokes when the Pleiadians arrive in their spacecraft?

Yes, they will have been screened. That's a good observation, as you can imagine it would be a poor start to public contact if people are dying of fright. The Pleiadians will suggest to the government beforehand to provide them with a list of reporters they wish to have on hand, and they will be scanned to make sure they will not be literally scared to death by the appearance of a flying saucer. They will want everything to be perfectly smooth.

Will a TV program be beamed to us soon announcing the presence of extraterrestrials?

Naturally, this has been considered, but I think you will see that the first real contact will be what I mentioned before — in Europe, live — although covered by the TV networks around the world. A TV program just will not have the effect that the live event will have. So I don't see this happening, although the idea has been bandied about extensively.

The Pleiadian Mission

Antura, can you provide me with a little more detail of what the Pleiadians plan to do in 2015, assuming that is still a "go."

It is still a "go," as you say. There will be a small group of Pleiadians who will set up a point of public contact with cameras rolling, I believe you say. This will take place in Europe.

Will they also go to other countries after this revelation?

Yes, according to who invites them, they will travel the world and meet with other governments over a period of a few weeks. This will even include the United States.

You say this will be over several weeks and not just a one-stop?

Quite so. More and more information will be released as reporters for news organizations and other people ask more and more questions.

✳   ✳   ✳

[Author's Note: A number of articles were published after I had received the previous information, containing everything from statements that the Pleiadians were backing off the 2015 date to a report that President Obama was about to sit down with a delegation from the Sirius star system! Others forecasted that they would not be coming in our lifetime. In the light of all this speculation, I thought I should ask the following question.]

Has the 2015 contact with the Pleiadians been changed? What is the real story?

There has been much confusion about this contact, even among the various channels, as they are called. But no, the date remains the same and, in fact, it has been somewhat more solidified as you continue to make progress. The Pleiadians will be first. The first contact will not be from the Sirius system. To answer your next question: Yes, there are some of our people that do look much closer to humans than, say, I do, but not as close as the Pleiadians.

We in the Federation have all agreed that first public contact will be with the Pleiadians, and yes, it will be around that 2015 timetable. Contact with governments will continue to go on, even though the leaders of those countries know nothing about it. We hark back to the previous statements given to you that the time is coming when many secrets will be revealed. They will not be able to keep the lid on it, to use one of your expressions.

But again, my colleagues and I will be coming a couple of years after that first contact, as things settle down, and a great deal of information will be given to the general public so that we can be accepted. That will be an exciting but somewhat tumultuous time for many people with religious views, contrary to actuality.

A Pleiadian in a channeled article seems to suggest that they are backing off contacting us in 2015. Is that true?

There definitely continues to be a lively discussion about when to contact you, but so far 2015 is still penciled in, to use a phrase of yours, as the date the Pleiadians will make first contact. Keep in mind that you have some enormous changes ahead, not the least of which will be your change of focus from the third to the fifth dimension. It will be the lowest degree of the fifth dimension, but it will still be a jump. Many things will begin to change rapidly for you after that while other changes will come slowly.

To answer your question again, contact in 2015 is still a "go," but this date will be monitored as you progress each year toward that date. Naturally, we all hope that date holds, as you will take a large leap at that time. Your progress will be accelerated, and you will make more progress in, say, five or ten years than you have in the past 100. It will be an amazing time!

After the First Visit

Antura, please explain a little more about the Pleiadians' visit. First, how long will they stay?

Not too long the first time. Let's say, for your purposes, over a month — but still a short time considering.

I assume there will be additional visits from them before anyone else arrives?

Quite so. There will be at least three or four visits, each one providing more and more information about a huge range of subjects.

What exactly will take place in the two years you have mentioned after the first public contact by the Pleiadians and your visit?

Well, after the excitement and fear initially settles down a little — and really this will take months if not the full two years — there will be some presents, shall we call them, given to your governments. These will be low-level instruments and other devices that your scientists perhaps had not thought of yet. These will be spoon-fed to you, as again, you are supposed to make these advances and again, they will be kept very low-tech so as not to interfere with this process.

There will be more explanations of who we all are and how you fit into the scheme of things and how important you are, even though you are not advanced technologically. These explanations will take months for the Earth population to absorb, and hundreds of questions will be asked and answered. It will be much more on the diplomatic side and for the first-contact people to handle than for any scientific breakthroughs.

Then I assume they be able to reveal their involvement and the Federation's involvement in our creation and history?

Yes, quite a bit. This will shock many of those who have refused to believe there could be life on other planets, much less that we had a hand in your creation. It will be a hard pill to swallow, shall we say, for those people who believed all of creation happened just a few thousand years ago.

How will they be able to convince the public in general about our actual history?

Their methods will include visuals that will put any of your historical films to shame, as they will be actual footage of real events in your path. Naturally, this will be released slowly in order to be better absorbed. The Pleiadians are quite good at first contact, and we all know you extremely well. They will lay out your history step by step.

Besides officials, will there be any grassroots contacts by the Pleiadians?

Certainly there will be, just as there will be from us. There are certain individuals who have already been informed that they will be meeting their forefathers, shall we call them.

Will this take place starting with the very first visit?

Yes, to a certain extent, but more in their second and third visits. This way there is a greater spreading of the word of what is taking place — not just through announcements by officials and coverage by news organizations.

How many Pleiadians live on Earth now, if any?

A few. Their mission is to be more understanding of the Earth Experiment.

How many Pleiadians are there on Earth at any given time mingling with Earth people?

Due to the lower density of the third dimension, not nearly as many as you might expect. They must wear protective gear, as is the case with us, although it is not perceptible to you; the extreme negativity just cannot be tolerated for very long. So their trips to the surface are fairly short — just a few hours, if needed. Their instruments, as well as ours, are so advanced that they do not need to mingle that much. Keep in mind that they — and we — have been doing this observation work for thousands of years.

How many inhabited planets are there in the Pleiades?

Quite a few — certainly several hundred. The Pleiades have a large variety of planets of just about every type you can imagine.

Antura, during the Pleiadians' first contact or series of contacts, will they explain that their society is over a billion years old (if this is correct), or will they be a little vague?

More on the vague side, as you have guessed. Even saying their society is over a million years old or five million years old will stretch the understanding of the general public and their beliefs. After all, you only have records dating back several thousand years. They will spoon-feed this information, if you will, for public consumption.

Will the Pleiadians explain timelines, and if not, then who will? And when will that be done?

Definitely not in the first couple of visits. That would be way too much for the average person on Earth to absorb. They will eventually get around to explaining it as simply as possible. They might even refer to your book, but that has not been decided yet. It will be the Pleiadians and not our group or another group. Trust has to be instilled, you see.

Who will be second — your group or another?

There will be another group prior to our visit. Again, they will have a much more human-like appearance than we do in order not to upset the population too much. But they will begin to also introduce other humanoids with different appearances at that time.

Will your group come after them?

Yes, although it will come just after another visit from the Pleiadians to announce our imminent arrival.

Will you arrive in 2017 too?

Yes, we wish to space these arrivals out so that there are at least three to four months at a minimum between visits so that the information imparted can be absorbed.

Will the second group to make an appearance be the Arcturians?

No, it will be another group.

A group from Orion?

Closer, but not them.

Are the Zetas the second group to visit Earth after 2015?

Yes. I know you will question why, but they want to explain that themselves as well as why they were in such a dire situation to need to abduct people in order to save their society by creating hybrids. They will profusely apologize, of course, but they will also trot out the hybrids to show the success of the project. They will also bring other humanoids with them too.

How will the Zetas be able to handle the negative backlash from people who feel they were abducted and abused, plus those who recall being either the father or mother of the hybrids?

Yes, it will be a complicated matter, although the Zetas will say the right things and will ask for forgiveness. They will volunteer to have these people open up their memory banks and remember details that were frightening at that time, and they will show why they had to alter their memories. Few on Earth will want to see the beings they parented, but those requests will be taken into consideration as they appear.

CHAPTER 11

SIRIAN CONTACT IN 2017

After the projected 2015 visit, when do you think you'll be coming?

Not too long after that — certainly within two to three years from that date. You are progressing at a much faster rate than was anticipated, which is fantastic. We are very proud and amazed at how fast you are progressing, even though it does not appear that way to you in your daily lives.

Antura, will you or anyone else on the ship be contacting governmental authorities or scientists on Earth during your visit?

Yes, there will be governmental contact by those of us who specialize in that type of contact. I, as I have mentioned before, do contacts more on a grassroots level — still very important for our studies and for your benefit, as we do not want to seem elitist by only dealing with governments or the scientific community. Again, it's passing on and explaining who we are, and that we are a peaceful society.

We need to have the general population understand why we're here and that we wish you no harm and you should not be frightened of us. That is all part of my job and the jobs of the other two contactors, as you call us. Our job is just as important, if not more so, than the people working on governmental or scientific levels. You'll see what I mean, and we can have more discussions — and we will — before 2017.

The Other Contactees

I assume that your other two contacts will be in different countries than mine?

Quite so. One is in Asia and the other one is in Europe. A wide variety, you would say.

Are they members of our soul cluster (see glossary) group too?

Yes and no — one is and one isn't. I have spent many previous lives with the one who is not; I know that one and its soul group quite well.

Then we have one more in our soul group incarnated on Earth right now?

Quite so. The person is living a life in — let's see if you can get this — Italy. Yes, you are close.

How long have you been in contact with them?

A little longer than I've been in contact with you. They have been in contact spiritually, shall we say, for quite a long time. They are not like you, having had a normal business life, shall we say for brevity's sake.

Regarding the other contactee you said was in Italy, or at least close to there, did you actually mean Italy, France, Greece, or another neighboring country?

Yes, a neighboring country close to Italy.

Then is it France?

Yes, but close to Italy.

Okay, Antura, does our soul cluster member live in France near the Italian border, or in Italy itself?

No, you have it now. The soul cluster member, as you call it, lives in the southern part of France near the Italian border. I know you resisted this, as you travel to that area and have traveled there many times for your business, but that person lives not too far away from Cannes, where you go. You've actually visited the place where this person lives during your vacation side trips.

It would be nice to meet that person if I get the chance, Antura.

Perhaps we can arrange that — we'll see.

Since the other contactee, as I understand it, is located in Asia and is not a member of our soul cluster, why did you or why are you making contact with this male or female?

She is female. You are the only male I will contact and meet with. The other two are females. And to answer your question, this woman in Asia was very open to contact with an ET or alien, and so I have been in contact ever since.

Was the first contact made initially to an upper timeline?

Yes, excellent question. After that, I simply went down the line, so to speak, communicating with each timeline expression of the soul fragment, shall we say.

In which Asian country does the third contactee live? Is it Japan?

No.

Taiwan?

Yes, that's correct.

So as not to leave this, it's not in Burma, Japan, China, Malaysia, the Philippines, or Indonesia?

No. You have the correct country. Stick with Taiwan. I realize it might seem surprising, but her soul contract called for her to begin this work at a very early age.

Will the other two contactees on your list write books? If not, how will they spread the word?

Yes, both will write and speak about their experiences.

Are both doing books right now?

No, they have not started their books yet. Those will come in the future.

Have either of the two you will visit published any books yet?

One has. But they are both also influential with or through their friends. Our goal, you see, is to have more people accept our different appearance and know that, even though we look quite different than the Pleiadians, we come in peace. We wish to assist you, as much as we are allowed, to become members of the Federation one day. I am an ambassador in that respect, you see, although just in the grassroots variety, as you say.

It is my understanding that you will be in contact with the other two people — the two contactees — all the way down to timelines 1 through 4. Is that correct?

Quite so. Again, they have struggled to receive these communications, but they have had years to develop these abilities, compared to your much more recent ability to communicate just since 2005. So you might say they were wired to do this early in life, just as you are aware of, let's say, people who are termed psychics who began as children.

You were veiled in a way, as it is in your soul plan to experience business, international travel, and the film distribution business, as this knowledge will assist you in getting the word out about our arrival to a much greater audience in a shorter length of time than the other two contactees are able to accomplish. Their books will come more after the fact, although certainly your experiences with me will result in another book. But it will also lead to videos that will be widely disseminated; I can assure you. We are quite certain that millions of people will view these.

What term do you use for contactors and contactees, Antura?

I know I have said those were your terms, but that works for you and for us, so there is no need to begin using another term.

When you're on your 2017 trip, besides working through conversations with all three contactees on all the different timelines, do you also work on contacts or prior contacts on other planets to fill your day?

No, my days are filled with studying Earth — the past, the present, and the immediate future, shall we say. There is a great deal of preparation that I do for these talks or conversations with you on your various timelines, along with my talks with the other two contactees. I must review each of your lives up to this point.

But still I must point out again that my life is quite a bit less stressful than your lives on Earth. We have much more time to relax. We don't go, go, go all day. And I probably put in greater hours than well over half our population, as this upcoming trip is so important. Everything must work perfectly.

Details of the Visits

Have the months been chosen yet for the visits in 2015 and 2017, or is this still fluid?

Certainly summertime in this hemisphere will be best from both our standpoints. Closer than that, I cannot or will not say. It could change, so ask me as we get closer to those years.

Will any of the other beings from your planet be on the mothership with you when I arrive on board?

Yes, one species. Naturally, I will be pleased to introduce you when you arrive.

When you pick us up, will you wear a toga or more formal wear?

Slightly more formal but not my complete formal attire that I would wear to, say, a conference. I know you don't expect it, but our first meeting I should dress up just a little, don't you think?

I suppose, but I'll probably be wearing jeans.

That's fine. You will wear what is normally considered casual on Earth.

Will there be other Earthlings on the mothership when we arrive on board?

Yes, perhaps a couple. They will not be my contactees, you understand, but they might be the charges of another of the grassroots person like me. Perhaps there will be scientists or even government representatives, although these people might be there for only several hours and not days as you will be.

As we get closer to that time, my colleagues and I will work out the schedules for everyone to know who will be on board, for what length of time, and when. Obviously, we must have sufficient facilities, including sleeping accommodations and toilet facilities for everyone to be comfortable. We will have the most humans we've had on board the mothership in thousands of years, and great planning is going into making every human's stay enjoyable.

What will you be allowed to present to us or tell us or show us?

Just the basics, shall we say. We do not want to overload your people with knowledge of our scientific achievements, as that would create fear and a feeling of being less worthy,. We do not want you to feel that way. You are very important to this whole universe, so you must be made to feel this way and understand what you will contribute to all of us. You are very unique in the universe, and we're thrilled that we will be able to make contact with you soon.

How long will your mission to Earth last?

Not too long the first time. Times will be set up for further contact and for your scientists to visit, and so on. It is very complex, and we are going to be very patient because we've done this many times in the past.

How many people will you be able to see on your trip to Earth? Will it be private or public?

That is still in the planning stages, as you would say. It partially or even wholly depends on Earth's progress during these next few years as to whether we can be a little more public or must keep everything under wraps, as you would say. Your progress has been great just in the last few years. We were not even planning to arrive as soon as we are now, you see.

When you arrive, will you dip into and out of time in order to maximize your visit, or will the visitations take place with the various timelines in what we call vertical time?

No, as you guessed, we can dip into and out of time in order that our appearance on Earth does not seem to drag on.

Could you do it in vertical time if you wished? Could you have the Pleiadians delay each announcement until you have completed your visits with a particular timeline?

Yes, but there is no need. We can dip into and out of these short time windows, shall we call them. Certainly there will be just a little of both involved — the timing of the Pleiadian announcement and the entry into a particular timeline. On the surface, these are complex maneuvers but not when you've been doing them a long time.

I assume you may have a list of twenty-nine or so people from timelines eleven down to one to visit?

You're quite correct. It will be an extremely busy time, but that's my job, and I will enjoy it tremendously, you see, as it will be an exciting time not only for Earth people but all over the Federation and expanding out all over the universe.

I hope your enthusiasm lasts all the way down to my timeline, Antura.

Yes, certainly it will, if not more so, as we know what a struggle it has been for you and timeline 5 to communicate. Your efforts are admirable.

The Fifth Focus

Will you have to lower your vibrational rate to our level when you come?

Yes, but not nearly as much as if we were to come today. You will be making that shift to the lower level, or frequency, of the fifth dimension before we come. This will open up so much for you as a people. You have only the tiniest understanding of this at this time. Things will be so much easier for everyone who stays around in the next few years.

Regarding the fifth-dimensional level that we will first be on, I assume it will be the lowest rung, or degree, of that dimension. And I assume that's why it will be much easier for you to drop down to that level than it is to drop all the way down to a third-dimensional level?

Absolutely. There is virtually no comparison. Yes, we are at a much higher fifth-dimensional level than you will be in the beginning, but the difference is much less noticeable than when I drop down to the third-dimensional level. We can't stay at that level for long periods without adequate protection, shall we call it — devices to help or assist us.

Have you ever visited Earth in your present life?

No, not yet. Yes, I know you thought I might have. I have much material and reports to absorb from the many visits we have made to Earth. We do have a team there, even as we speak, gathering information constantly — readings and such that you're not aware of yet in your development. So we know precisely, and I repeat precisely, where you are in this development so that we will know when it is time for us to arrive and make ourselves known publicly.

Is this craft above or under the ocean at the present time?

Yes, a good question. The craft can be in both places, as sometimes it is easier for us to cloak ourselves under the sea than above. So it all depends on what readings and tests we're doing. And we do converse with your cetaceans, you know.

Visiting Earth

When you come to visit, will you visit with our whales and dolphins?

Yes, most certainly. We will confer with them and a few other sea creatures to see how their lives are and any problems they have.

Do mermaids, as we call them, actually still exist in Earth's oceans?

Quite so, but they are at depths far below what you can travel to at this time — at least in normal submarines, shall we say. They do keep to themselves and have openings in the sea floor to their habitats. They learned long ago to avoid humans, as they did lose some of their people to overzealous sailors who wished to capture them. They learned their lesson and have a very low profile today.

I assume you will contact them?

Yes, but it will be more of a courtesy call. You are the focus of our studies — contacting you and others.

After our first contact, how often will you visit Earth?

I will actually visit several times, as we must slowly introduce ourselves to more and more people. It will be a very slow process, as we must handle you with kid gloves — I believe you have that saying. We will be very gentle and as unobtrusive as possible.

It will take many years for the religions of the world to accept the fact that there are other people in the universe. That must be handled very delicately, you see. Plus, those in power in various countries will be concerned that their power will be taken away. So we must assure them that they can continue to rule or run their countries in the manner they see fit, although those who really abuse their power will have greatly lessened by the time we arrive after 2012.

Are your instruments sensitive enough to detect Earth changes weeks, months, or even years in advance?

Yes and no. We do have sensitive geological instruments that can detect minute changes in a planet's interior, but that can only go so far. We can take those instrument readings and make a very good prediction about what will happen and be very close to the actual results, but there is still just a little unknown factor there. But to answer your question: Yes, we do have these types of instruments.

I've been told that there is now a brand-new society that comes from a planet that blew itself up and inhabits the lowest rungs of third focus on Earth. Will you visit them too?

Yes, but briefly. They are not ready for too much contact yet. They need literally thousands of years of experience in order to move up in degrees.

Do they have eleven or twelve timelines too?

No, just you do — the Explorer Race. That society is not part of the Earth Experiment.

Bringing the Family

If I bring a digital camera with me, how could it be recharged?

A very simple conversion device will be used, one that has unlimited energy. This will be arranged well before you step on board the craft.

Here is a question you've probably been asked by me in timelines 7 and 8 and may have hoped I would ask or knew I would someday ask. With the whirlwind of activity I see before me during my short stay of one week or so — however much you allow — it would seem easier if I brought along my own camera crew, consisting of my family. So what did you tell 7 and 8 and what will you now tell me?

Yes, actually this is a good idea. I have agreed in principle to it, depending on whether they will agree to accompany you. They probably will, because they have been prepped, you might say, by their guardian angels as part of their soul contracts and those probabilities your own guardian angel has talked about before. So the answer will be yes, you can bring them along if they choose to come. We see a definite increase in your and their abilities to handle our meeting. Naturally, all the details will be worked out as we get closer to the time. But yes, your idea that your younger children will be able to carry on your work for many years after is solid.

I certainly think it will be a win-win situation for your purposes, Antura, as my daughter is a film school graduate. Are either of my children from the Sirius B system?

No, they are not, but we have contacted their planets, and they have no problem with them being involved and acting as your support.

When was the use of my family to be my camera crew first considered, Antura — from the very beginning or did it develop late?

Certainly, when we laid out this plan for you, we had to take into consideration the best way for you to have the experience and then be able to convey to others what you saw and experienced. Therefore this was an option early on, depending on whether you chose to involve only your wife or decided to expand your idea of what you feel you can accomplish.

Will the Pleiadians or Zetas invite people on board, including journalists who will also be filming?

Actually, no. Your visit will be the first involving extensive filming or video recording. The Pleiadians and Zetas will have a few on board, but those will be just people who will take photos and a few short clips with their smart phones.

Will we be able to have one or two of our group used in a demonstration of how your scanners work in your medical facility on the mothership?

Quite so. We think that would be a good idea as part of showing the overall workings of the mothership.

When we are filming you and other members of the crew who will speak to us, the audio will have no problem in picking up your voice, will it?

Not in the least. It will hear the sound generated just as if I am saying the words in English myself, and the same will be true for my colleagues.

Then no one will need to send thought packets?

No, their thoughts will be translated by the device into sounds you can hear.

When on board the mothership, how will we adjust our time there? Will we remain more or less on Earth time, or will we adjust to universal time?

Good question. No, during the time you are on board the craft, you will remain on Earth time. If you spent an extensive time on board, then yes, your body would adjust. You will feel more refreshed in this environment.

I hope we will not be so excited we can't sleep.

That may be a problem, but if so, there are natural things we can do to relax your bodies. The beds are designed to put you into a restful sleep, as they are far in advance of what you sleep on now.

Okay, Antura. I think I understand my role more in relation to what you will be doing regarding first contact.

Yes, I understand you had an eye-opening moment there, when you put things together.

Yes, that's a good way of describing it.

Group Meeting?

When you visit, is there a possibility of meeting with a group of Earth People?

Not necessarily, but there has been talk or discussion of having a group meeting during anyone wishing to attend can do so.

Now I would like to make a request. I understand that your normal first contacts on a grassroots level are quite limited, but I think you will find that by the time we meet, there will be a great desire for more information from many people. But I do think that perhaps making an appearance with three or four of the humanoids with a group such as I spoke to recently would be quite welcomed and would greatly increase the accep-tance factor for people in general. Certainly we could make it on an "if you wish to see and speak basis," but these people are really drawn to this, don't you think, Antura?

Yes, I understand, and certainly we have had some discussion in that direction and no decision has been made yet. And yes, after tuning into your talk, I tend to agree with you that there is great interest from these people. Perhaps something could be arranged in which we might check the people out and let you know who would become too frightened — even though on the surface, they claim it would be no problem — and those who would be thrilled to meet with us and ask us questions to take back and pass along to their group and eventually the world.

We realize that making our first public contact with you at this time will be completely different from any contact we have made before, although we, as you can imagine, have had a lot of experience over a few million years with different beings. You are unique, through being veiled, and we do not wish to frighten you.

When you return us to Earth, will you be able to drop us, let's say, fifteen minutes after we left?

Quite so. It will seem to anyone that might possibly be there — I know that's why you're asking — that you just took a little ride. But again, I will remind you that the decision on whether you can invite people and who you can invite has not been decided yet. Much progress must be made in the coming years and months so that we will not frighten anyone.

[Author's Note: Antura can read me like a book!]

CHAPTER 12

THE
MOTHERSHIP

When you come to Earth, what is the size of your spaceship?

As you have heard, these craft are monstrous by your standards. Yes, they are well over one mile in length. Keep in mind that we do have a large crew with many different tasks to perform. And the craft must be capable of carrying multiple life forms, shall we say, as we often have our neighbors or even other Federation guests on the craft. All of these neighbors and guests must be accommodated according to their individual needs, and you might not even be able to imagine how different we can all be from each other. Yet we all have these common interests, so the craft can be changed in a short time to accommodate almost any form of life, within certain limitations. Certainly the being you were thinking of would not be able to be accommodated due to its size.

[Author's Note: Here, Antura is referring to the being who spread out over a large area of its world. See chapter 6.]

How long does it take to travel from your planet to Earth, since we're a little over eight light-years away?

Not long. We do use space portals, as you call them, or stargates is the other popular name, I believe. So the time is almost instantaneous. We're here and then we're there, not too far from Earth, so we quickly move from that location into orbit around Earth.

Do your spaceships cloak themselves by using a sophisticated version of the light-bending materials announced here by our scientists or something totally different, like changing to a different dimensional degree?

Good question. We actually use both, depending on the circumstances. If we are in an area and do not wish to frighten the local population, we will use a more advanced version of what your scientists are just now learning how to construct and use. If we are under scrutiny by warships or war craft that would try and attack us, we simply leave the point of the dial, [Antura's humorous way of saying "depart this frequency"] if you will, knowing that it is impossible for any of your ships to follow us yet.

How many people —or should I say beings? — will be on that ship when it comes to Earth?

There will be a fairly large contingent. Let's see if you can receive the number — more on the order of 1,000.

How many beings crew the large craft, Antura?

We typically have over 700 crew members and sometimes as many as 900. I know those figures sound large, and we can go over those numbers again in the future, but yes, the spacecraft is quite capable of carrying that large a crew along with passengers.

Will all these beings be from your planet, a few planets nearby, the Sirius star system, or even beyond that?

Our contingent of beings, shall we say, will come from a wide area — many from other star systems. We are a most friendly group, as you can imagine, and we come from all over the Federation of planets.

How many beings is the ship capable of carrying, let's say, in normal comfort?

Certainly the figure is well beyond 1,000. Keep in mind that some of the beings are quite small and require little space while some require a significant amount of space. There are more smaller beings than large ones, so many can be easily and comfortably accommodated.

When you come here in that big mothership with that large crew, obviously it is not coming just for you to speak to me. Will many of the other crew members and passengers be in contact with Earth humans here too?

Good question. Yes and no. Several of them are working with other earthlings just as I am with you and two other people, and they will have their meetings too, you see. Some of the crew will be in contact with your known leaders, and some of the crew members will be in contact with scientists and other learned persons. At that time, the initial contact will be over and the various governments will have appointed people to work with us both scientifically and on a sort of political level as well, as there will be many discussions on how all this will proceed.

Don't forget this has been done hundreds of thousands of times before with other worlds, so you might say we do have the experience needed to bring you along. But in your case, it will be at a very slow rate indeed, as we still want you to learn things on your own in perhaps unique ways that we have not considered before. These motherships, as you have guessed, have made these trips many thousands of times, but we just keep them cloaked so that they do not frighten your population. Even these contacts will still require that we keep the ship cloaked to a certain extent.

Location of the Mothership

How many miles out in space does the mothership lie?

Good question. The mothership on duty right now sits about fifty miles out in space — far enough out but close enough to deploy the scout craft.

So it is fifty and not, say 100 miles out?

No, much closer to fifty miles, but remember that it is cloaked.

That seems awfully close. I would have expected something like 1,000 miles.

Again, there is no need for such distance, as we are invisible to both the naked eye and to any radar or instruments. We shift slightly in frequency.

Just to be sure I'm receiving correctly, the International Space Station is 220 kilometers above Earth — over 135 miles. Then the mothership is less than half that distance above Earth?

Quite so. We are able to maintain our orbit, unlike your unmanned satellites and the Space Station, through slight adjustments. It might seem as if we should be much farther away, but it is so much easier to take these readings from much closer to the surface. It is also easier to deploy the scout craft to do their missions much nearer to the surface.

Does the mothership remain stationary or does it orbit Earth?

Again, a fine question. It does tend to slowly orbit so that constant readings can be done.

Where is the mothership that you'll be coming in right now? Docked on one of the Federation worlds, exploring the universe, maybe somewhere close to Earth?

There you go! Its current mission is close by you. The crew is taking measurements and such. You are the most important place in the universe right now, and therefore more resources, shall we say, are being devoted to your planetary studies. We want your integration into the Federation in the coming years to be seamless. Of course, that is why I will be on the ship when it comes again in a few years' time. My 800-plus lives give me real insight in understanding Earth humans, having been one so many times myself, just as you'll do someday in your next life.

Since the mothership is there now, will it have to return to pick you and others up, or will you come in another mothership?

Yes, we will be in another mothership and will relieve this ship of its duty, you might say. We keep a mothership in the area on a constant basis these days, as it will not be too long even in your Earth years before first contact is made by the Pleiadians, and then it will be our turn.

How long has this mothership been near Earth on its latest mission?

For quite some time, more than ten Earth years. That is not so long in universal time, we shall call it.

How long can these motherships be gone without having to be resupplied? Or are the ships capable of making food and water and whatever substances are needed for the crew's survival?

It can stay on duty, if you will, for several hundred years of your time, as it is capable of generating most of the sustenance needed for our bodies. There are machines in these ships that do work you will not discover for hundreds of years. But that's the way it is supposed to happen.

Have you been to Earth on one of your motherships in the past?

Of course, but only once, as I needed to do some research in preparation for speaking with you on your different timelines. I needed to be more knowledgeable about this time period and now have much more understanding of what is going on in your world at the present time.

So you are not on the mothership right now, are you?

No, I am not, but that was a good question.

The Mothership's Mission

What sort of readings are you able to do on Earth to know our vibrational rate, and what other instruments can you describe for me that I would understand?

Yes, that is a tall order or request. Our instruments are able to calculate very precisely what rate your Earth society is vibrating on. It is not just one instrument but several readings that are put together and analyzed. These instruments are simply far beyond your knowledge at the present time. As an example, they can analyze how you affect trees and animals around you. We do this quite benevolently, you see, as there is no need to take anyone aboard our spaceships to perform this analysis — we can do it from a distance.

There are so many other instruments that we could cover — instruments to assist someone if they are accidentally hurt in some manner, instruments to test food sources, instruments to analyze air but in much more depth than you can do now, plus instruments for water analysis, rock and mineral analysis, and so on.

In your ship, can you travel forward or backward in time?

Yes, of course we can.

Then have you already visited me in the future?

No, not yet. We have much work to do, and you have even more work to do before that happens. It must therefore stay on a linear track. Your future is still quite fluid and forming with many potentialities.

How many pilots does it take to fly your spaceship?

As you can guess, it takes someone quite familiar with computers — our kind and not yours, I might add — who is capable of setting in the right coordinates and then setting the course. On arrival through the portal, they do have the job of personally guiding the ship, if need be, to the exact location it needs to go to in that star system. So to answer your question, there are several people on board with this capability. Time must be allowed for their sleep time, meditation, eating, and so on.

Does the ship require engineers to take care of any engines or machinery? And what about navigators?

Navigation is handled by the computers; I am using your words now. But there is a need for different types of engineers to handle very complex machinery and functions.

Is the unit that powers your spaceships in the center of the ship?

Yes, for the majority of time, it would be fairly centrally located.

Is the ship alive?

Yes, in a way; that's a good question. The ship does have a personality of its own. Keep in mind that all the molecules and atomic particles that make up the ship agreed to do so and were not forced to be part of the ship if they did not wish to be, so the ship itself is a very loving entity in that it wants to be a ship.

How do you request the metal that wants to be spaceships in order to build these ships?

Again, this goes back to attunement. We attune ourselves with the ore, and certain parts of the ore respond to our request.

The Appearance of the Mothership

Is the mothership oval, cigar-shaped, or round in appearance?

It is more a giant oval in appearance.

Is the reason that there are many different shapes because these motherships come from different worlds?

Exactly, and some come from different eras too. Keep in mind that time is an illusion for you and is not the same elsewhere, so a craft from a million years ago your time could conceivably visit you.

Was this mothership constructed in space, on the ground, or in the water?

Good question. All the construction was easily accomplished out in space, as you call it. Needless to say, the capabilities to do this type of construction is far in advance of what you are capable of doing now, but then we do have a few million years on you.

Do the motherships ever land or do they just hover?

They are so large that it is easier to keep them in the air than to find a mile-wide landing strip for them. They do have the capability to land, but we rarely exercise it.

How long ago was the mothership constructed?

Several thousand years ago your time. Again, these ships want to be ships, so they do not wear out in the same way as your vehicles do. As new ways of moving between worlds or new inventions are introduced, it is fairly easy to add to or update the inside of the mothership.

Can a mothership heal itself if the hull is punctured? And has the hull of this mothership ever been punctured?

Never in its whole existence has that been a problem. Potential dangers are seen so far in advance through the instruments that those dangers are avoided or a force field is put up.

But if you are near a world with heavy space traffic, how are you able to avoid the other spacecraft?

Yes, there is a great deal of local traffic around our worlds, but we have no need of a traffic control as you do. These computer systems are so far advanced that they choose the perfect route to take, avoiding not only the spacecraft in the area we're headed to but also all the spacecraft they know will show up through portals, heading for that area or landing spot. Our ship may make a ninety-degree turn if it sees some small local craft wandering about on a pleasure trip. We don't notice the motion of such turns, thanks to these advanced hulls and magnetics.

Does the mothership you will be on have the appearance of a long tube, or will it have another appearance, such as the spaceship I saw in the District 9 *movie?*

No, the mothership will be much smoother than the one you saw in that movie. This mothership is long and, yes, somewhat boomerang shaped, but it is certainly nothing like the ones that are portrayed in most of your movies.

Do your motherships have lights, and if so, are they just lights or do they perform some other function?

That's a good question. Yes, there are lights ringing the motherships, and they perform several tasks beyond just illumination. They are part of the propulsion system, plus they are also part of a force field for the ship, should we care to activate it.

Does the mothership have a name, and is it made of organic materials?

Yes, it does have a name, but it will be a little difficult for you, so let's not mess with your reception. It is made of organic material.

You said before that the mothership is aware. But does it actually think and respond to your commands or even to mental commands from the pilot of the ship?

Yes, it does have the capability to respond to the pilot's commands as they think them. There is quite a close relationship between the pilots and the ship. There are no controls needed; the pilot just tunes into the level of awareness of the ship. Pilots obviously undergo training not only to be pilots but also to practice tuning into the awareness of the ship — this does take quite a bit of training.

What do your computers do that ours do not, Antura?

Oh, keep in mind that we have had computers, as you call them, for millions of years, so ours are so much more advanced in their capabilities that it would take hours for us to cover the differences. These are almost living beings in a way. Certainly they can instantly anticipate our demands and questions and give us much more complete information than yours are capable of giving you at this time. Naturally, their speed is also instantaneous. And, their size is about that of the head of a needle, in your terms.

Can you communicate with the mothership itself? Is it cognizant?

Not in the way you think. It has a cognizance, but that is more on a level of awareness, if I can use that description.

So to summarize, motherships have the capacities or abilities to do things themselves. But crew members have to perform certain tasks to prepare for a voyage?

Yes, there you have it. The motherships have many more capabilities than anything you can imagine at the present time, but the ships work in conjunction with the desires and wishes of their crews so that all personnel feel at home during the years they are away from their families and friends. And I will say the crews are made up so that no species ever feels as if it is alone.

Sections of the Mothership

How tall are the ceilings in motherships? Can they accommodate larger heights?

Absolutely. Certainly there are rooms or sections of motherships that have much smaller ceiling heights, but motherships in general are designed to accommodate a wide range of beings, from the smallest to the largest.

Are there sections of motherships with the correct atmosphere for different varieties of beings on board? Is this standard, and can you elaborate?

Yes, this is quite standard on most motherships. There is the oxygen-nitrogen atmosphere, but there are others such as methane and even more exotic atmospheres that different beings breathe. They are accommodated in the best way they can be. Obviously, some sections are much smaller than others, and the divisions will vary from mothership to mothership, according to who is on board.

Naturally, when a group in one atmosphere wishes to communicate in person with groups in other atmospheres on board, adjustments must be made in the form of breathing apparatus and suits of a special construction, but that is fairly easily accomplished these days. We have had, after all, several million years to perfect how to handle and accommodate different species on the same ship.

These living spaces are adjusted to the personal needs of each species regarding sleeping, eating, waste disposal, and so on. That's another reason why these motherships are so huge — they must accommodate a large variety of beings at any given time. We don't stay to ourselves as you do even in your cities or countries. Still there are those societies we encounter in our travels that do not wish to associate or assimilate with other cultures, and we honor their requests and move on. You will have those experiences too when your Explorer Race goes visiting other cultures.

Does your craft have a large pool for your relaxation and perhaps regeneration?

Yes, of course. I'm happy that you thought of that. We do have such a tank or pool that we can utilize to relax and regenerate ourselves. It functions similarly to a place of meditation.

Regarding your medical facility on board the mothership, when crew members are in-jured, do you manipulate their DNA or use magnetics, crystals, or something else?

Yes, the closest description I can give you is that DNA is manipulated to instantly heal a wound, for example. The medical instruments are so far ahead of what you have now that it is difficult to describe to you. Advanced computers are used to scan the person or being's body, noting its DNA structure, and then it is simply a matter of setting the dials — although there are no literal dials, as this is done automatically — and the being is instantly healed.

Provisions for the Voyage

Antura, on a long voyage on a mothership, are there provisions for everyone stored in the bowels of the ship, or are they manufactured on board by certain machines, I'll call them?

That's a very good question. We have machines capable of producing any food item you can imagine — and many you cannot imagine — on the menu for each species of travelers. And, I will add, you cannot really tell the difference, as these machines or devices are perfect reproducers of the foodstuffs.

Do the machines that replicate the food on board the motherships simply replicate the DNA profile or signature — whatever it's called — of the desired food and produce it in perhaps a similar way to our 3D printing systems, or is it instantaneous?

Yes, it does use what you call the DNA profile, but as you guessed, it is done instantly. There is no use of lasers or any similar devices to create the food. This might be considered, perhaps, the next step for you in the process, but when you are able to list the DNA signatures, or profiles, in a computer, you are one step closer to creating food instantly.

I assume we will have that capability by the time we take off for the stars ourselves?

Quite so. You could not carry enough provisions to be gone several years, as you will on such journeys.

Earthlings on the Mothership

During the thousands of years that this mothership you will be arriving in has been in existence, has it been the host to other earthlings before?

Oh yes, quite a few. These ranged from ordinary individuals to leaders and scientists of their day. A number of them had to have their short-term memories deluded or erased, as they would have suffered damage to their psyches.

How far back did these events happen?

Certainly all the way back to Atlantis. This mothership, you understand, has been around a long time. I know you think it has only been around a few thousand years, but it has existed for many thousands of years in your time. There was much more contact between us and earthlings, but it was decided after Atlantis to really limit these visits, and the Earth Directive came into being so that you would evolve at your own pace.

Antura, returning to your comment about deluding or deleting peoples' memories of their visits to the mothership, what were the beings on board trying to accomplish?

They were doing some studies of the human body that were best done in a controlled environment. Plus, there were visits in which they wanted to show someone an idea to use back on Earth without it being a conscious memory. We are only allowed a little leeway in working with earthlings up to this time period, and there were things we were allowed to suggest — but only in a subliminal way.

Plus, in many cases, the people brought on board were frightened of the experience, as they had not accepted the idea that there could be other intelligent beings in the universe. They were conditioned, shall we say, to reject that idea. So it was best to delete these memories or bury them so that it would be very difficult for them to remember. This was done at a time when we had less knowledge about you than we do now.

What goals will we hope to accomplish by our visit and others' visits to your mother-ship in the upcoming years?

After the initial contact by the Pleiadians, there will be a great shift in understanding and acceptance. It will be much easier for us to introduce concepts and various other beings to you and to others. You will write about these experiences in turn and will assist in helping everyone to accept other forms of intelligent beings and humanoids so that we will be able to work more closely with earthlings in the coming years.

Again, I have said before, we will spoon-feed you just small bits of information at a time, as you are supposed to learn many things on your own without our assistance. We just wish to point you in the right direction, to use your vernacular.

Getting to Earth

When you come here in the mothership, will you use one of our portals or one on another planet close by?

No, we will use an Earth portal and then move away from the planet itself. It would make no sense to use another farther away when we can just use a portal in your own backyard, so to speak.

Some of the images that appear in videos and on film of spacecraft seem ghostly in appearance or wispy and not solid.

Yes, these are not always spacecraft but sometimes actual beings. But others can be spacecraft. There is no set answer when you have thousands, if not millions, of possibilities.

Could you comment on "beamships" attracting themselves to stars for propulsion?

Certainly that was one way to travel in the distant past, and you may go through that phase yourselves, but learning how to travel through those folds of space will be what we believe to be the easiest and fastest way to travel.

The Number of Motherships Monitoring Earth

How many motherships are in this solar system, observing and taking readings of Earth at the present time?

Quite a few. Certainly over thirty that I know about.

How many ships are from other universes?

Again, quite a few — fifteen or twenty.

Is that part of the thirty number you mentioned?

Yes, it is.

Have you been on any of the other motherships from other universes?

Yes, on occasion. Their motherships can be radically different from ours. The beings who are on these ships are even more different from the ones we see in this universe. And I can assure you that we have an enormous variety.

Have you been instructed about what information you cannot provide me?

Yes, but so far we have not touched on those areas, so it should not really concern you at this time. Obviously, it would be things like propulsion — more detailed workings of certain instruments that you are not really too interested in since you're not a scientist in this life.

Tom's Stay on the Mothership

How long will I be allowed to stay in the mothership, and will my wife, Dena, be allowed to come with me?

Good questions. Certainly if you wish to spend a week or so of your time on board, you will be accommodated. As a first contact person, normally we make contact and then leave. But in your case, you are much more advanced than the species we typically deal with when we are making early contact, so certainly this will be taken into consideration. I don't think you will have a problem adjusting with the exception of having a breathing apparatus attached to you, which will be almost imperceptible.

As for Dena, she may or may not accompany you. This will be her decision, but I understand that you wish her to experience these things in preparation for your next life together in the 3400 AD era. *[Author's Note: Antura is referring to me and my wife's next lives on Earth as space pilots of one of seventeen Earth starships.]* And to answer the question floating around your brain: Yes, you will be shown anything you wish, as we know you are not scientifically oriented and would not take what you see and reproduce it. We are allowed to show you but not give you technical knowledge. If you mention some of these things in your writing, it will be as if a person was writing a science-fiction book; you will simply be presenting what you have been shown.

Will we be able to download information about the Sirius planets through those skull-caps you have mentioned before, or must we ask each individual being on the mothership about his or her world the old-fashioned way?

Yes, you may consider it old-fashioned — and certainly we do from our perspective — but we cannot just give you the information in an emersion session. You must explore and ask your own questions, and you will not learn many things about the planets in our star system, and you will ask questions that we did not think to include information about.

We want to give you a taste of these planets — not their whole recorded histories. That will not only be for you to discover and learn about but for the many people who will come after you. You will be the first on this timeline to learn general information about us. Your writing and speaking will then cause many others to wish to learn more. You will be the catalyst.

Will we be able to see the other motherships traveling in orbit around Earth from your mothership?

Yes, although they will be small images that will need to be enlarged, as they are not that close together. There are many satellites that you humans have put up around Earth, but they are not too visible to the naked eye unless one passes by, you see. It's the same even with mile-long motherships.

Then will we just visit your mothership, or will we go calling on any other?

No, at this time, you are only scheduled to explore this mothership and ask questions and learn about the planets in my solar system. And since there are so many, it will be just an initial introduction to these societies.

Will I be able to take pictures, Antura?

Yes, you may, and no, we will not limit where you can take them with a couple of exceptions.

Have I ever been on this ship in a past life?

Good question! Yes you have in fact — several times, so when you visit, there will be a déjà vu feeling. At certain times, you will probably feel that you know which way to turn.

Are there any video records of me on this ship?

Probably, but we are not so concerned about capturing every moment through pictures or video as you are. Again, this comes from having very long lives of several hundred years — over 1,000 years. Things do not seem so urgent, you see. That is a huge difference between the vast majority of ETs, as you call us, and Earth humans. Because you live such short lives, you must cram everything into a very narrow level of time.

The Total Number of Federation Motherships

How many motherships are there in the Federation, Antura?

Hundreds. Keep in mind that, being in space for millions of years, there was time to construct hundreds, if not thousands, of craft. Even Earth will have, as you know from your conversations with your guardian angel, seventeen of these craft by the 3400 AD era, and that's just a few hundred years from now. So you can see how there would be lots of craft in the space lanes, as you call them, doing explorations.

✳   ✳   ✳

Can you give me a more definite number of how many federation ships are there to-day, Antura?

We're not ready to do that yet; we do not wish to create fear in the population. That's why there will be only that one ship uncloaked in 2015 coming to Earth to begin your introduction — the public's introduction anyway — to the fact that there are billions of beings out here in the Federation to welcome you and to begin explaining what purpose Earth will have as a catalyst for us all.

Antura, I've recently seen some huge numbers in regard to how many ships are monitoring Earth and people. Can you give me those numbers? One report said 16,000.

That is not at all accurate. Certainly there are now a few dozen in total, as you are currently in the year when this first disclosure happens. But there are certainly not the numbers you suggest or read. Many of the ships share their data with whoever wants it, so not so many ships are needed, you see.

Gravity and Air in the Mothership

What gravity do you keep on the mothership, and do your force field devices further adjust?

We keep a light gravity — let's say the equivalent gravity of Mars, not Earth.

What is the difference in the gravity your shipmates are accustomed to handling on the mothership?

Excellent question. Certainly these suits we wear have a number of purposes besides breathing atmosphere, and adjustment of gravity is one of them. It is done through magnetics. As a people, you have so much more to learn about magnetics. It's as if you have taken only one or two steps on a long walk, to use that analogy. Plus, when various shipmates are in their own living accommodations, the actual living quarters can be adjusted to any atmosphere and any gravity they wish. This capability is literally thousands of years in your future. You will not need to have this when you begin visiting other star systems, so your spaceships will have but one gravity.

On the mothership, what temperature does the ship run at in the public or common areas?

An interesting question. It is kept at a mild temperature, and since there will be those on board used to much hotter and colder temperatures, their suit apparatus, we will call it, automatically adjusts to changes.

What is the air comprised of?

The air is much more as you will find it on many other planets. I will let your scientists take those readings themselves for their own discoveries. But I can assure you the air that you will breathe will be at exactly Earth quality, perhaps just a little above.

How will that be accomplished? We will not wear bubble suits, will we?

Not at all. Systems were developed long, long ago to give you a mini–force field, shall we call it, in which you will breathe an atmosphere that is comfortable to you, along with keeping you at a temperature that is comfortable.

CHAPTER 13

THE MOTHERSHIP'S CREW

Antura, how many other people from your planet will be coming with you?

Only a couple. Again, although the crew is large, everyone has different jobs, you see, so one must have a good reason to be on the ship. There are hundreds of applicants, and they can accommodate only so many. Therefore, they try to spread it out to include representatives from as many planets as possible — it is very diplomatic, you might say.

So to answer another possible question: Yes, there will be a large variety of beings or people, or whatever term you wish to use, from humanoids to many other types of beings. Everyone wants to be here for the action, and I feel fortunate to be chosen to go.

How many different species of humanoids will there be on the spaceship?

A minimum of ten different species of humanoids will make the trip — perhaps more, as that has not been fully worked out as of yet. There is still time, you see.

How small are the smallest beings you have worked with on the mothership?

Oh let's see, smaller than a tiny bird in your calculations.

Aboard the Mothership

Will there be any bird-type species on the ship?

Of yes, there will be quite a few, although some you would only barely recognize as having bird-type features. They will be quite different in some instances.

How large will the birds be?

Certainly there will be a few that will be, say, half your size.

Do the bird beings on board the ship have beaks?

Yes, in some cases but not all. And, I'll add, they are smaller.

What about the equivalent of whales, dolphins, or other fish-type species?

Yes, a few. But as you can imagine, being away from their oceans is quite difficult, so they tend to stay where they are. They are not the explorer-type visitors, shall we say. They rely on us, the amphibians who can represent them, as we know them quite well and can communicate and pass messages along, if you will, to their brothers in your seas.

What species have I not mentioned?

Certainly the insect-type species. It is still hard for you — in general here — to think of insect-type species as being fully intelligent creatures, which they are. So we will have several of their species with us. And there are a couple of species that defy categorization.

Will there be any Arcturians on your spaceship when you come to visit us?

Yes, just a few. They will have a minor presence, as they have their own ships and make these trips with contingents from their areas.

Will there be sentient plant forms on your ship when you come?

Quite so. I realize it is difficult to include plants as you know them, but there are quite advanced sentient plant forms throughout the galaxy and universe. So they will be represented, although you may not recognize them as such — at least not all of them.

What appearance do these plant beings have on board the mothership? Are they humanoid in appearance?

Somewhat. You can tell they have a plant-type appearance, but they are so exotic, it is difficult to describe them to you.

Do they live just on light?

Quite so. They must use special equipment that duplicates the energy they receive from their own planet's sun while on board.

Do they have arms and legs?

Yes, of a type. Again, they would seem almost vine-like to you.

How tall are the plant beings?

They can grow to enormous heights, but the plant beings on board will be a little smaller than, say, a normal Earth being.

You said they appear to have sort of vines for appendages. Are they multiple or more humanoid in appearance?

No, more multiple, as they are quite unique. And their skin structure, to answer you next question, is smooth and green — not a brilliant green, but much more subdued.

Do they have a head, eyes, nose, and mouth?

Yes, but again, not anything like you've seen.

What will be the height of the tallest being on your mothership?

For this trip, no higher than, say, seven feet.

How large will the insect species be on the mothership I will visit?

Much larger than on Earth but still smaller than a humanoid.

What would we equate them to on Earth, or are they so different that there could be no comparison? And do they have wings?

No wings, but there are those that do have them. Their appendages do have that insect "flavor."

How tall are the insect beings?

Smaller than, say, both of us.

Do they have multiple appendages like insects on Earth?

Just four to six on average.

Do they walk upright or on their multiple appendages?

There you have it. They move about on these appendages — legs, you call them.

Do they have shells?

No, this protection is not so needed.

Eyes and mouth?

Yes, but with an insect "flavor."

What about any large mammals such as we have on Earth like the lions or tigers?

No, they are part of the cat family and will be represented, just not in that form.

What species are the pilots?

They vary, as you can imagine, since several are needed to run the ship at all times of day or night.

Will there be reptilians on the ship?

Yes, a couple, although they tend to keep to themselves, as there was the little matter of wars a long time ago. As I said, we are peaceful now and have been for over a million years, but some types of beings don't mix very well.

The reptilians are our friends now, you see, but there is a history in the past. We do have good relations with them now, and as I said, they will have a couple of representatives, as they have their reptilian brothers on your planet as well, and they will glean information from communicating with these brothers during our stay.

Why would two reptilians be on a Sirian spacecraft?

They were invited to join the expedition and accepted. They will be studying their own ensouled people to see how they are doing.

Are these humanoids or another type of reptilian?

No they are humanoids — small in stature but definitely reptilian.

How tall will these reptilians be?

Below the normal human height. They will not look as menacing as some of their brothers who are quite tall — yes, fourteen to fifteen feet in height would be correct for their upper ends.

Is the reptilian race from Orion or from some other star system?

Yes, a few are from the Orion sector, but the majority are from farther away. There are other star systems that teem with a reptilian "flavor," shall we say. It was at one time a difficult confrontation, but now we are peaceful. And no, there really isn't an underlying current of mistrust, as you might be concerned about. We are good friends now.

Remember that there are thousands, if not millions, of intelligent life forms in the universe, and we are simply waiting until our big jump when the earthlings arrive — the Explorer Race.

Then I assume I will get to meet them too?

Quite so. You will have full access to the spacecraft and will meet everyone on board and ask any questions you wish.

It seems to me, Antura, adjusting to the different appearances of the crew will perhaps be the most challenging for an earthling?

We think so, but we are hopeful much more information comes out about them in the next four years, so it will not be such a surprise when you arrive.

What will take place in the next four years that will contribute to making people less fearful before you arrive?

A large number of events. The Russians will describe the appearance of the aliens or ETs they have met with over a period of many years. Certainly it will make all the world papers, some printing more information than others. Then comes the contacts first with the Pleiadians and then the Zetas who will trot out several different models, shall we say, each perhaps a little more exotic than the last.

You and I will not stop our conversations, just because the book will be finished and published. You'll have many more questions flooding in from those who buy your books, to the point I anticipate a second book. You will be receiving me much better over that time period, so I'll be able to give you better details on what your readers ask.

Antura, have you ever found humanoids in the universe with one eye — what we call Cyclops in our legends?

Oh yes. There are several different species — shall we call them humanoids? — with just one eye. Yes, they look a little strange even to me, but they are for the most part, very gentle beings. They will be encountered by the Explorer Race in your travels.

Will there be any of these beings on board your ship when you come?

Not this time or on that planned trip, but perhaps in the future. They will seem to be truly so strange as to be a little unnerving to you with your legends and stories of monsters.

Eating, Facilities, and Work

How does everyone order their food on the motherships — sort of cafeteria style or by pushing buttons or through voice recognition? How does this work with so many species of beings?

Yes, that's an excellent question. Each being is served through what we will term for now "voice" or "sound" or "tone" recognition, although it might have to be physical contact with a special ordering board. That's the best way to describe it. We do tend to have centers to eat, share stories and comradeship, and develop friendships with all manner of beings, you see.

However, there are personal issues here, and some species of beings prefer to eat by themselves, but they will come and be cordial during other parts of the day. So there are a wide variety of eating styles and modes, as you can imagine and even well beyond your imagination. Some do not even partake of food. They receive their sustenance through light and various rays that they must absorb. And some of the eating methods might not be too appetizing to all those on board.

How are toilet facilities set up on the motherships and the scout craft for those who require them?

These are easily set up according to the specific being's requirements. There are pop-in modules to handle any requests for devices stored on board, or if not, are brought on board before the ship leaves on its mission. Needless to say, there is a huge variety of this type of facility, depending on the size of the being, and many, many other factors.

I hope there will be facilities for Earth humans when you come to visit us.

Of course, everything will be arranged well in advance.

Does the mothership reconfigure its interior itself each time to accommodate different types of crew and guests, or is it done by the crew members?

Both. The mothership has great abilities to adjust on command, but some work is always needed for adjustments.

What other work is there in the ship?

Oh my, that might take hours to describe, but yes, there are beings who prepare food; beings who work as scientists, processing information gathered from the worlds we visit; and beings to run and service countless parts of the ship. There is a need, you see, for so many people on board.

When you're on the mothership, how do you know when your shift is over — when it is time for another being to take over?

The answer to this will be complicated for you, to be sure. There is a semblance of time but certainly not the same as on Earth. On the mothership, people come and go by simply telling their partner or partners in doing whatever studies they are involved in that they wish to be relieved. Much is done by advanced forms of computers, which allow us much free time to pursue our own interests and to be able to meditate at will.

Life is not as complicated for you. It is much slower in pace. Still, there are duties that have to be performed, and there are beings who volunteer to do them. We are a big happy family on the ship with few, if any, cross words between us.

Then the answer is that you do not really keep to any set schedules. Is my understanding correct?

Yes, although we do have specific duties that must be performed, because we take pride and enjoyment in doing what we do, it does not really seem like work.

Do the beings on board wear some type of suit with colors denoting their work or even planetary origin, or is it left up to the being to wear what it is accustomed to?

More the latter. You will find a huge variety of dress onboard the ship. They will not look anything like the crews of *Star Trek* but just slightly like the *Star Wars* presentations — only the different forms of life, not any uniforms.

Other Grassroots' Contactors

How many others of the crew on the mothership will be doing grassroots' contacts besides you?

Only two others will be doing the same type of contacts I will be doing.

Where are they from?

They're also from the Sirius B star system. They are humanoids like me and have close relationships with several people on Earth from the standpoint of soul clusters and such.

Are these land people, or are they water people — amphibians?

No, as you guessed, they are land people.

Will it be two or three humanoids?

Unless things change, it will be three.

I was going to ask you to describe the ten humanoids on the ship coming with you, so let's start with these three, if you will?

I'll try. Your reception is pretty good this morning.

So is the first one tall, medium height, or small in stature?

Yes, fairly tall, but not the fourteen or fifteen foot height. This one would be closer to seven feet in height and have a fair complexion. This one does have hair — more reddish brown in nature. He has wide eyes, a little smaller ears than those you have on Earth, a prominent nose, a smaller mouth, and yes, five fingers and toes — a little more to what a normal Earth being would look like.

What about the person's skin?

Yes, it is thicker than yours, and it has to be because of the sunlight.

Did I ask what type of planet this contactor is from?

No, you didn't. The one we previously spoke about comes from a land planet certainly more barren than this one, but people live underground much of the time to protect themselves from the sun's rays. You will find that, throughout the universe, people or beings adjust to their living conditions, just as they do here. But life is just not as hard overall as it is here on Earth with such extremes. This makes the Earth humans hardy, adaptable to all conditions. This is something that will come in handy when you begin your travels, first to the surrounding planets and then to the stars.

So let's take the next contactor. Is it a male or female?

Female, in this case. This is a job shared fairly equally between males and females, although there are categories that are neither. This person looks closer to the human species but has darker skin than the first contactor described — a very exotic looking being. She has black hair and normal limbs, shall we say. She is slighter in build, closer to my size. And she has green eyes — we will call them green for your purposes, as you almost do not have their color on Earth.

Is she from Sirius B?

Yes, exactly, from one of the twenty planets we have discussed before. Everyone on the ship will be from these planets with a couple of exceptions.

Is the third grassroots' contactor humanoid?

Yes, of course. And again, more like the way you look than, say, the way of my appearance.

Height?

The contractor is slightly over six feet in height with a little yellowish tint to the skin. Again, the skin is thicker than yours.

So two eyes and ears?

The third contactor has larger eyes, as those of most humanoids, and smaller ears, as with the other contactor we discussed before.

Fingers and toes?

Yes, but they are not the same number of digits. The nose is roughly the same size as yours, perhaps a little smaller. The mouth, again, is smaller. There is some hair growth but not much.

In our eyes, what will be the most unusual being on the ship?

I must say this with humor, but you will be flabbergasted to use your own words to describe the beings you will meet onboard. We have discussed before that there will be bird beings, reptilians, and yes, beings from the insect realm. You will be in sensory overload, to use your words again.

CHAPTER 14

THE MOTHERSHIP'S SCOUT CRAFT

Antura, do you have smaller scout-type craft, shall we call them, or does the ship just descend to whatever planet you are going to in whole?

We have done both. We do have the smaller craft so that we can do multiple studies or even one study across different parts of a planet at the same time. The mothership, as you call it, can remain in orbit and receive these transmissions from the smaller craft taking readings of many, many types that are beyond your understanding or capabilities at the present time.

Yes, that's one question I do have. Why will it take so many hundreds of years for us to learn these things, as I've been told that after my life in the 3400 AD era, I'll have a life 800 years before to explain what we'll be finding. Surely this information will be available to us long before that through our connections with you?

To a certain extent, but keep in mind that we are not allowed to give you too much. We can give you little bits and pieces, but you are to make your own discoveries as part of the Explorer Race.

You will make discoveries that we have yet to make, because you will not be so influenced by the past as we are, if that makes sense to you. Therefore, you will be allowed to rediscover or discover what we already know, but in a different way perhaps, which will be exciting to all of us watching this experiment.

How many of the scout ships does your mothership carry or hold?

Good question. Certainly twenty to thirty on average. Besides these scout craft, there are some people movers, shall we call them, that are like buses or airplanes in that they can hold larger numbers of people, but there are normally only two or three of those.

How large is the craft that you will take down to the surface of our planet, and how many does it hold?

Yes, these small craft, as you call them, are not large. Let's see if you can receive this, yes: forty feet in circumference is about right, not too much larger than that. It can hold five to eight comfortably, I would say.

Do your motherships and scout craft have the ability to create clouds, Antura, or is what we see just a holographic appearance?

Excellent question. It is quite easy to create a cloud formation to assist in cloaking our ships, although I know you will ask me why they do not appear more normal. The answer is that we want them to appear unusual to the population so that they will notice and wonder about the cloud formations. Naturally, we have the ability to create normal looking ones should we need to, and we have done this countless times in the past when we did not wish to be noticed or seen.

Since you said previously that the mothership is controlled by the pilots' mental instructions or communications, are the scout craft controlled in the same way? Or since there is a variety of people — beings — using these craft, do they just have manual controls?

These scout craft easily adapt to each being's thought processes so that if the pilots of these craft wish, they can simply order the craft to turn and go where they visually or mentally instruct. But some beings like the pleasure of controls, so those are available to use if anyone wishes.

Could these controls be changed to fit the size and appendages of the pilot?

Yes, that is easily accomplished by simply thinking or entering one's race.

Are your scout craft from the mothership round, triangle-shaped, or globular?

They would be the more classic round shape.

Do the scout craft sent out from the motherships have transparent glass, plastic, or alloy, or are all your observations done via some sort of images displayed inside the craft?

No, there are portals to view outside, but obviously they must be much stronger than glass or plastic. This alloy was developed over a long period of time, and your scientists will not discover how to do this for several hundred years, as we will not be allowed to give you this information. You must discover it yourselves.

I assume the scout craft have retractable legs?

Yes, and as you surmised, there are typically three for stability. They even have the ability to meld into the ground just a little for even more stability. You have probably seen photos taken in which these craft have landed and left significant marks on the soil or ground.

Are your scout craft able to hover, should you wish them to, just above the ground and not extend the landing gear?

Quite so, but under normal conditions, the scout craft landing gear will extend down to the surface. There are few times we would need to hover, and of course, it takes a pilot at the controls to keep it at that level. The landing gear can take just about any surface known. If the surface is fragile or the craft would sink for some reason, then it would hover, but we would probably stay on board. And to answer your next question, yes, we have instruments to tell us if the surface can hold the weight of the scout craft. These instruments read the conditions in a split second, so there is no waiting around for analysis.

Please describe your spacecraft door or portal. Does it drop down straight to the ground, or is it more of a ramp?

Actually more of a ramp — perhaps a little shorter than you have pictured or imagined but still easy to use. Even this can be modified, depending on the being using it. It is flexible in a way — you might say it has multiple settings.

How the Scout Craft Functions

What is the maximum speed a scout craft can attain not using a portal?

Extremely high speeds — well over 10,000 miles per hour.

Would they be able to travel at 20,000 miles per hour or faster?

Yes, but not so much above that without the need to use a portal.

Do the occupants know instantly that they are being watched and captured on film or video?

Yes, most of the time; they are showing off, as they are allowed to do. The ships are having fun, knowing many people will see them and several will record their presence.

How do the occupants of the scout craft know they are being watched and photographed in any way?

Readings are taken, and they are very accurate, down to individual people, so the scout craft pilots are quite aware from their instruments who is watching them or will be in a position to observe them. The instruments can read feelings and thoughts.

Speaking of these spacecraft in general, Antura, why is there no g-force inside the craft when you make abrupt turns? How do you nullify the gravitational force?

This all has to do with magnetics and force fields and such. These are things your scientists will learn as they began to study magnetics much more in the future. They have only found or discovered the tip of the iceberg, to use your terminology.

✷ ✷ ✷

[Author's Note: Later I asked for more information on the g-forces at work.]

Yes, this ability to null the gravitational g-force, I believe you call it, was developed many centuries ago, and you will eventually learn how to do this yourselves. I can't give you too much information, as this is another thing for your scientists to figure out how to do. But suffice to say, there are inner compartments, or layers of hull, that act as balancers to these sudden accelerations. I assure you this is very complex. It will take many hundreds of years for your scientists to duplicate.

How does the scout craft, and I'll add in "mothership," avoid all the space rocks, meteors, space garbage, and even satellites?

There's an easy answer for that. We certainly have equipment on board to avoid these objects — an advanced form of radar that automatically guides the ship to and from its destination. Keep in mind that we can also move up or down in frequency quite easily to avoid objects and even to avoid those who desire to chase us and shoot us out of the sky. So we have a variety of ways on board the spacecraft to accomplish this, and if the ship is in mortal danger, we can even use a portal to escape.

Antura, when — at what age — were you taught to pilot any sort of spacecraft, or is this something simply downloaded into a child's brain?

Good question. The information is initially downloaded through those skullcaps, but this is not done very early, because there is no pressure to do it. The child must want to learn this, and many have no interest in learning it. So after the information is downloaded, the children then take a short course in piloting the craft — hands on experience, if you will. But this can come at any young age — say, from ten or twenty years on up to fiftyish. Again, many are quite content to simply live and eventually work in the sea, and they have no interest in going to even a nearby planet.

Witch Mountain

Is the size of the scout craft depicted in the movie Race to Witch Mountain *the same, larger, or smaller than those carried by a typical mothercraft?*

There are actually a variety of sizes, depending on the origin of the mothership — which star system, galaxy, or even universe it came from. Keep in mind that you have visitors from other universes who wish to observe and take readings of this successful experiment, as it is called. So I can only answer that the craft you saw in that movie is somewhat smaller than the ones we use in our own mothership. You thought that I would say it was larger, but no, the scout craft have to be a little larger to hold sufficient personnel to accomplish whatever missions they are assigned.

In the movie, the girl could move objects mentally. Do your people do this?

Only rarely, as it is not necessary. Certainly you will find other civilizations, especially the Arcturians, who have developed that ability. Anything is possible, you will discover.

Does that include the ability the boy has in the movie to dematerialize?

Yes, quite so. That is normally done through the use of certain devices, but it is not something done every day by the normal being, say, at least not in our star system. Again, I return to the statement that Creator likes variety. Each of us develops abilities according to need. There are beings who developed this ability through necessity.

Was there any ET influence on the making of this film? I thought it was a good "preparation for landing" film, since it showed the alien kids as sweet people, although of course it had to have the hideous-looking bounty hunter.

Yes, they were depicted well. Our only influence was to mentally encourage those people in the film industry that now would be a good time to do a remake of the original film, as yes, we thought the same as you — the children were portrayed not as monsters but more like what you'll see when the Pleiadians arrive.

How did you know the size of the spacecraft depicted in Race to Witch Mountain *movie? Did you scan my memory bank, or were you able to somehow see the movie?*

Good question. Yes, I used a simple method to scan the image of the spacecraft that you were thinking of during our conversation. I honed in on that image. It is much easier, as we've discussed, to do this on a fifth-dimensional level than it is on a third-dimensional level.

Will Earth be given a small craft to practice with, and if so, when will that occur?

Not for some time — it won't be for quite a few years. Certainly it will be after our visit to you. It will depend on how we feel you are progressing in your acceptance of us. But yes, that time will come. At first, after you have gotten used to us, we will take those scientists and such to our worlds. Then there will come a time when we loan fairly simple craft to you. Soon there will be the next stage in which you construct your own craft, using principles that you have learned or were taught. Again, everything will be done at a fairly slow rate, as we wish to see what you might come up with that we have not thought of.

CHAPTER 15

TRANSLATION AND FORCE FIELD DEVICES

When we meet, Antura, will you speak with a voice, mental telepathy, or the translator device you have previously described?

It will be the device, as you call it. It will seem as if the words are coming out of my own mouth. These are very sophisticated translators that will allow the first contact people to communicate effortlessly with beings on a much lower developmental scale than Earth so that they feel as if they are speaking with a person from their own planet. We can take on the image of that being.

Are these devices external or internal?

External.

Are they the size of a computer chip, shall I say, or larger?

No, but you have the basic idea. They are quite small, as obviously over time, devices of any kind tend to grow smaller.

Are they self-sufficient, or are they connected to some type of computer device on board either the mothership or the spacecraft?

They are connected to both.

Do they operate via audio, brain waves, both, or in some other fashion?

They are capable of absorbing brain waves or functions, but they are also capable of interpreting any form of verbal and nonverbal communication.

That includes clicks, whistles, and other sounds of all types?

Quite so. Keep in mind that these devices, as you call them, have been developed over millions of years.

How much of a language must the translator capture before it is translated?

Again, this goes back to reading a being's brain waves. From there, it is simply a matter of identifying the syntax.[3] The translator is capable of translating millions of languages it has built up over time.

Does it feed brain waves to you, or do you hear it as audio?

It can do both, according to who is using the device. We don't even think about it, as it is so natural and easy to use.

I assume you have had one or more lives on Earth in an English-speaking country?

Quite so. I've had several, in fact.

Are you able to bring up a particular Earth language you spoke? Or is there no need to do this due to the use of your translation devices?

There you have it. Yes, during meditation, I can bring up one of the prior languages I spoke, but there really is no need because of the complete translation devices we have. As I have explained before, they are capable of reading brain waves and other minute idiosyncrasies of a language — any language in the universe. As a comparison, calculations done by hand just a few years ago — in relative time — are now done on your smart phones or computers. You would not return to the slow manual way unless your computer devices were not available, so it is the same with us and our translation devices.

When you use the translation device, do you continue to hear the sounds the being makes or are those sounds muffled so that all you hear are the words verbally or are they thought packets?

Certainly it would be distracting to continue to hear the other being's sounds, so we hear only words we understand. They are conveyed via a sound system, we will call it. And yes, the words are also received as thought packets. So it is a multi-listening device.

It would be very difficult to concentrate on what is being said if you could simultaneously hear the other being speak while you were hearing the translation — I am using a simplified description here. It would be quite disconcerting unless you practiced using it this way, as was done in the distant past before the translators were more fully developed. These translators went through various different models and upgrades over an extremely long time before the ones used today were created.

Then is this accomplished mentally or physically?

An excellent question. It is more mental, in a way, yet still physical. So you could say a mixture. After you use one of these devices one time, you don't even notice.

Is the voice you hear one that varies from being to being, or is it more or less the same tone?

No, it does vary, as it takes the essence of the language and yet is modified. And yes, if you are speaking to several members of the same species, you will be able to tell which being has spoken.

---

3 For those of you who, like me, did not know what the word "syntax" meant above, Webster's Dictionary defines syntax as "an arrangement of words as elements in a sentence to show their relationship to one another" and "the organization and relationship of word groups, phrases, clauses, and sentences."

Is there any society in the universe this does not work on?

Not as far as we've found.

Will the Pleiadians use the translator devices, or will they speak multiple languages?

No, they will also use the translator devices.

How does the translator work when there are beings with multiple languages all together? If one person speaks to another in his or her own language, then that language would be the primary language. Therefore, would the other beings still hear it in their own language?

Exactly. Each translating device has the ability to translate simultaneously into whatever language the beings speak. As an example, if one person spoke French and the others German, Spanish, and English, then all would hear each conversation between members of the group in their own language. These devices are capable of handling hundreds of languages all at the same time.

Please explain the difference between a translation device and telepathy skills.

This is somewhat complicated for your understanding. A translation device is just that — a device that picks up brain waves and all sorts of audio and visual stimulus as we have discussed before. The skill of telepathic communication must rely on two people — and there can be more that tune into the conversation, as you are well aware — who transmit these thought particles to each other over any distance, even across the universe. And yes, this leads to your next question about inner space and hyperspace. This is the space those thought particles travel through instantly on their way to and from these individuals, just as you and I are doing right now. It will be many, many years before your Earth scientists are able to really understand this inner space and the voids, we will call them.

I assume this is the same space a spacecraft travels through when you go through a portal and come out a long distance away?

Quite so, but it is not exactly the same. This is very difficult to explain in three-dimensional terms, but as we have discussed before, there are limits to these portals that make it impossible to travel across the universe in one jump. It must be multiple jumps, similar to your Southwest Airlines that I gave you as a comparison before. There are no limits on thought particles being transmitted across the universe. This gives you a little hint that there are different forces at work here.

Force Field Devices

I assume you have some advanced device that will allow you not to have to wear a spacesuit here on Earth, or are you an oxygen breather?

We do have devices that allow us to be present in almost any atmosphere that you could imagine.

Is there something physical that you put on to adjust to different gravities and air and even to go out in space? Or is there a device that has been developed that does this for you when you turn it on?

Exactly. We do not have to put on any suits of any kind, not even the type that are transparent in nature that you might have thought of originally. Our science is so developed that a device was created or invented to adjust to all conditions relative to what is considered normal to each individual. Good question.

Regarding the device you wear to give you a force field and the correct air to breathe, does it act as a complete spacesuit, allowing you to exist in the harshest conditions on planets and even in space itself?

Yes, these devices are so powerful that we can exist at almost every temperature degree variant there is, from the hottest to the coldest and, yes, even in what you term the vacuum of space.

How does the force field device adjust for the variance in temperature at which two beings of the same species, using earthlings as one example, feel most comfortable?

This can be controlled both manually and automatically, as these force fields can detect slight variations in the comfort levels of different people wearing them.

Are these tiny devices — both the force field device and, I assume, a separate device for translation — attached to your body, as you would not want them to fall off? You previously said they were the size of a pinhead?

Yes, certainly it is not a glue. When activated, it naturally attaches to your body. The person who asked the question suggested magnetically, and in a way, it is magnetic. Once attached, it will not become unattached until you turn it off with a verbal or mental command.

Can someone on a different world touch you with your force field on and not disrupt it?

Yes and no. It depends on the action, so I cannot give a general answer. Most of the time, it would still protect us, but again, it depends on the action.

Are we talking about violent actions or just a touch from, say, me laying my hand on your arm?

Yes, we are speaking about violent actions, as there are some who this force field is not able to repel — but only a very few. Harsh environments are no problem for this force field.

Does the force field protect you on other planets against any diseases?

Yes, it completely blocks out any harmful spores, plant life, and any types of germs that would be harmful to our bodies.

What about on your planet?

We are quite healthy and need no special devices, as our bodies are quite compatible with our environment.

Is your force field and your translation device combined into one unit, or are they two?

Good question. I knew you would figure that out. They are combined into one unit, as the unit is quite capable of millions of tasks all at the same time. If you have a billion years on hand, you can devise some amazing devices to make life easier.

■●CHAPTER 16●■

PORTALS

Author's Note: Before I ever began asking Antura about portals, or as some people call them "stargates," I posed a number of questions to Gaia, the soul of Earth. As I've been told, each planet and star has its own soul to run things. So first are questions addressed to Gaia, then Antura.

Gaia, are there portals on or in Earth to other dimensions or across vast amounts of space?

Yes, we do have portals for those beings to transport themselves without fear of interruption, or worse, to and from Earth and other dimensions and realities. They are able to cross the timelines into other timelines and into and out of this one, plus they can physically move to and from their ships that are hovering nearby, cloaked so that they are not seen in your dimension. There is a vast amount of traffic, as you call it, to and fro. A good question for an early bird!

Are there many of these portals or just a few?

There are a number both under and above the surface of Earth. I have allowed these to be constructed by very advanced beings who have your best interests at heart. We do not allow the dark beings to use these facilities, which answers a possible question you might have asked. They must be safe for all to use without fear of running into something that would be detrimental.

Is there still a portal in the Sedona area?

Yes, there is, in Boynton Canyon and in one of the other canyons nearby.

How do portals work?

Ah, this is a difficult question to answer, as it is steeped in knowledge that you as humans are not yet at a stage to understand it. A simple explanation would be that people — and obviously spaceships and so forth — go through these portals and wind up in another place. Several portals can be used to make your way across the universe.

Why can't one portal take you all the way?

It is like having to make stops in various cities in an airplane that is not a direct flight. There are no portals that can take you from here to the end, or the other side, of the universe. These portals connect specific areas of a galaxy so that you do not have to travel through what you call the vacuum of space.

Why does it require such a higher vibration on our end, or for that matter, anyone else in the universe?

It's because the vibrations of the portals are set so that they are tuned to a specific frequency that will not allow third-dimensional beings to travel through these portals.

Are there souls in charge of these portals?

Oh, absolutely, yes. They are the keepers of these portals and they keep them tuned, so to speak, to the right frequency so that no one is lost during their travels through the portals.

I read that a portal was damaged during a war across the universe somewhere. Did that happen?

Yes, quite so. The warring factions, I will call them, on a small planet decided to collect revenue for passing through their portal, which is absolutely forbidden. The portal was damaged and was unusable for a long time afterward.

To make this clearer, in order to travel great distances in the universe, you have to portal hop?

Exactly. These are short cuts across vast distances of space, but they can only go so far. They have their limits, which your physicists will one day understand.

If a third-dimensional soul cannot go through a portal, then how have we had exchanges of scientists in the past?

Ah, an interesting question. As you guessed, their vibrational rates are raised when they enter the spacecraft that transports them to the other world. It can easily be done by these people, as they are far advanced with their technology. That is how they are able to come to third-dimensional Earth, as they must lower their own vibrations so that they can visit the third dimension. That is an easy answer when you think about what those people do in order to visit you.

Are these only for fourth- and fifth-dimensional beings and objects, or are they utilized in higher dimensions too?

They are used by higher dimensions — but not much higher, as by that point they are lightbeings, shall we say.

Are portals utilized to travel in time, or is that only something relevant to Earth?

Certainly it is much more relevant to Earth. As you have read, you have been visited by beings from the same planetary system who are far different in their time. For example, a young Arcturian as compared to an older race of Arcturians.

These different worlds have their own time, even though it is different from Earth time. So once they gain the ability to jump through portals, it continues from that point forward.

Did the Creator make these portals or humanoids?

They were created. Or at least they were part of creation, as the Creator knew there had to be ways for people on one side of the universe to learn about others.

With that in mind, are there multiple portals to the next galaxy, say, or is there just one from each galaxy to another?

Ah, a deep question. I will say for the moment that there are multiple portals. But that does not cover the full implications nor can I answer that completely for you, as there are quantum mechanics involved that have not been discovered yet by your scientists, and I would not want to take away the fun and excitement of discovery from them one day.

When were they first used?

Of course, it was millions of years ago in your time, as I know you knew. But your question pertains more to how they knew to use them, so I will say that their spiritual advisors passed along the information. Keep in mind that, in other societies in the universe, spirit is not separated from science, shall we say, but they work together to attain knowledge for the population. That will happen to you one day here on Earth as scientists realize that much information can be gathered from spiritual contemplation, just as I give you this information now. As I have said before, you have to ask me. I will give you knowledge of the cosmos — knowledge of creation and such — but you must ask. I cannot spoon-feed you this information, although it may seem like I am doing that even now. It is only because you asked.

So their spiritual advisors told their scientists of the day what to look for and how to utilize these portals.

That is correct. Otherwise it would have just remained an abnormality in the fabric of their worlds and the universe.

Gaia, you said some time ago that portals will allow us to travel from one place in a galaxy to another without traveling through the vacuum of space. Yet don't most scientists look at space as a vacuum? Are you saying there is a difference between space in a galaxy and space outside it?

Let's see if you can receive this. Space is not a vacuum; space in galaxies such as our Milky Way is made up of a substance that your scientists will discover in the not too distant future. Certainly space outside this universe is a vacuum. Again, they will discover this but much later in time, you see. So there is a substance, but your instruments can't really measure it yet. That's one of the thrilling finds for your scientists to discover, so I will not take too much away from their discovery by revealing it in advance — just small hints for you and your readers.

Then when we portal-hop, we are traveling in that substance?

Yes, in a way.

But is that substance present between galaxies?

Yes it is. It is not a pure vacuum, you see.

An astronaut reported that space smells to him and he can smell it when people come in from a space walk. Is that the substance you speak of, and why does it smell?

A good question. Yes, it is that substance, and again, your scientists will discover in the coming years what that substance is. Again, not to give anything away, but it does have a makeup that can be analyzed in laboratories, which naturally will have to be located in space.

So if I wish to portal-hop to, say, the Sombrero Galaxy, as we call it, how many portal jumps would it take?

Quite a few, as that particular galaxy is far away from you. It would take — let's see if you can receive this number — over ten portal jumps to reach that faraway galaxy.

Since Earth is at the edge of the Milky Way Galaxy, do people portal-hop through here often on their way to another galaxy or just to another part of the Milky Way Galaxy?

Good question. Your portals are used to go to a variety of places both in the galaxy and outside of it. You will discover in the coming years that you are a jumping-off place for those traveling to other galaxies. It was designed this way so that after you discover how to hop from portal to portal, you can say that you are in a terminal with portals going to many other locations.

Gaia, are the portals here on Earth used for specific destinations, or are they used for multiple destinations?

An excellent question. They go to multiple destinations with some limits. They are not programmed, shall we say, to go to every destination, but once the pilot of a spacecraft, for example, arrives at one of these portals, he has a list of destinations that are possible to travel or hop to that he can enter in the ship's computers, and then the ship will go to that destination.

Is the list for each portal long, and does it vary? Will some portals have more destinations than others?

Yes, the number of destinations a portal serves does vary from portal to portal.

How many times on average are our portals used each day?

Dozens of times — dozens. As I said before, you are a jumping-off place, so there is much traffic through here, just as there is at a train station with a large number of tracks coming in and an even larger number going out where beings are coming and going all the time.

I'm not sure if I can receive this, but what about the portals associated with, say, Sedona. Where do they go?

Quite far you see — even to another universe, certainly to another galaxy and certainly to several places or worlds in this galaxy.

How close is the next universe to us, Gaia?

Fairly close. A few will be identified with a little help from your friendly ETs. Your scientists, as you've just read, are peering into the far reaches of this universe and are seeing that there is a gaseous substance that they are saying makes up what they call the web that holds everything together. They have many more revelations of this nature ahead of them, thanks to the work of the Hubble telescope.

Back to the subject of portals, does every planet in our solar system have one or more portals?

In my experience and understanding, yes. Every planet has a portal. Sometimes a planet will have many portals, as we have discussed, but certainly a minimum of one is given by the Creator.

I wasn't sure what you would answer on that one, Gaia, as I thought with all the trillions of possibilities, there might be some that did not have a portal.

Yes, it would seem that way, but again, in your voyages across the universe when earthlings begin to explore the stars, you will find not only great variety but even some similarities too. Portals are just one of those similarities you will find.

Does each planet have as many as Earth does?

No. They are not main hubs, shall we say, as Earth is. Some only have one or two and others have a number but not sixty-plus as Earth does. Some have a few — less than ten but more than the one or two you thought they might have.

Are the portals — those sixty we have discussed before — on the surface of Earth, beneath the surface, or just above?

Excellent question. They are just at the surface — the large majority. There are a couple inside, but the majority of the sixty are at the surface or just barely above it.

I thought they would be a little higher?

No. Close to the surface.

When someone wishes to visit Mars, they don't really have to come through an Earth portal, do they?

Yes and no. It depends on where they originate from, as again portals are like highways. You sometimes have to take a highway to one city and then connect with another to a different city.

Yes, I can visualize that. In turn, are there some people who would have to go through a Mars portal in order to visit us — or, for that matter, one of the other planet's portals?

Yes, exactly. Again, these portals are like a maze of highways, each with its own destinations.

In three-dimensional terms, the database that holds all this information must be massive. Are all the portals in the universe known? Do they have to be known? That's a little confusing.

Yes, there are databases, as you call them, that hold all this information that can be tapped into at any time. A spacecraft traveling from one point to another does not have to carry this information with it. It is available for anyone to tap into for directions, you see, from one point to another.

Is this information kept by one society? Or is it kept by, say, the Central Sun Alcyone, or if not there, then where?

Good question. No, it is kept in several places and by several different societies, works, and star systems. Each shares its knowledge with all who wish to access it.

That brings me to another question. Do the reptilians have access to this knowledge, and are they free and clear and able to travel at will through any of the Federation portals, or must they request permission?

Another excellent question. Naturally, during the space war, they were prevented from having this information, although that did not stop them. They found ways around this blockade, if you will, as they had planned this in advance. They knew where most of the portals were from the beginning. After peace was achieved, they were allowed — and are still allowed — to utilize these portals without supervision, shall we say. That was part of the peace process. Again, they don't tend to travel extensively through the Federation portals but can do so at any time.

The Ins and Outs of Portals

Antura, how do individuals transport themselves? Do you have beams as in "Beam me up, Scotty" of the Star Trek *series days? Or is it through portals or how is it done?*

Good question. There are a variety of ways that people can be transported from one place to another — even from one planet to another. We don't always have to travel in a spacecraft. There are portals that allow individuals to travel through them. And yes, we do have the capability of beaming someone or some things up to a ship if need be.

Are they just energy portals, or are there any portals such as the ones portrayed in our Stargate SG-1 *series?*

No, there are only energy portals. It is a very third-dimensional concept to give portals a physical form. The actual portals are simply a change of focus, or an energy window allowing quick movement from one side of the universe to another, although there might be several portal jumps, shall we call them, necessary to reach the particular place you are going.

Are there, or were there, any portals of any kind in Egypt?

Yes, there were and still are one or more portals in this ancient land. One includes the great pyramid — a small but significant one.

Have any sea-going Earth vessels accidentally gone through a portal in the Bermuda Triangle or perhaps another location on Earth?

No. As I have mentioned before, third-dimensional people and things must have their vibrations raised in order to enter these portals. That is for your protection and ours, as on a third-dimensional level, it would be very difficult for you to enter a higher dimension.

Were there any ships whose vibrational level was raised enough for them to pass through?

Only on one or two occasions when there were lives at stake and there was angelic intervention, shall we call it.

Antura, when you travel to these other worlds and galaxies, do you have the same problem that we humans will have when we go on extended trips to other worlds — the matter of losing days, weeks, or months in your home world?

We do not lose nearly as much time as you will. We've already been doing this for millions of years, you see, whereas in that 3400 AD era, it will still be relatively new for you. Even using portals, as you will, there will be a loss of days, as remember Earth is on a different time system than universal time. It is extremely difficult to explain with your third-dimension concepts, but universal time and Earth time work at different rates. Remember, time for you has sped up, but when you go to the stars, you will be experiencing universal time which is different.

Therefore to answer your question: Yes, I lose a little time but not too much, you see. So if the trip is extended, perhaps I would lose a month of my time on my planet — not so much, you see. This is the best answer I can provide you at this time, as this is something for a quantum physics scientist, and even they don't truly understand the difference yet nor will they for a long time to come.

There seems to be a contradiction about space portals. I've been told on one hand that portal jumps can only be made in space ships and, on the other, that individuals can portal jump. Please clear this up for me.

I'll try. The answer to both is yes. Spaceships do move through portals, but some types of portals can be used with the right kind of equipment for individuals to move through them. If these individuals were naked, shall we say, they would not be able to make a jump. It requires equipment far beyond your knowledge and understanding today. It still has to do with magnetism.

I just read a piece by Robert Shapiro in the Sedona Journal of Emergence! *in which he channeled a Pleiadian explorer who uses an older spacecraft for his explorations.[4] He does not use portals to jump but goes from mothership to mothership hitching rides. Why is that?*

There are all types of beings out there, and you could call this particular one a Renaissance man in a way. Certainly these portals are for everyone's use, but some prefer not to use them, as is the case with this person. His is a leisurely journey of exploration, and as he himself noted, he flies an older spacecraft that he calls his jalopy because he's in no hurry to get somewhere. He enjoys his interactions with the crews of the motherships perhaps more than his explorations of new worlds, although he certainly does his job, just slower than perhaps you or I would wish to.

Is the figure of sixty portals correct for Earth, Antura?

Yes, that is almost the exact number of space portals. And yes, some are programmed, shall we say, to go even outside this universe while others go just inside the solar system and still others go to far parts of the galaxy. Again, these will be great discoveries for Earth scientists, but that is pretty far in the future.

Are portals the same as what scientists call wormholes?

Not exactly. They have the general concept but not the particulars. Portals are shortcuts across the universe, but scientists are still off on how they actually work. It will take many years of study on their part to discover how portals actually work.

Do you have to travel to these portals in order to use them?

Not exactly. We are able to program our ships to immediately access a particular portal without physically traveling to the portal as long as, let's say, we are in the area.

Antura, on the subject of portals, do you somehow fold space before going through a portal?

No, it is not accomplished in that manner. There are already folds in space that we are able to take advantage of in portal-hopping. That's why we cannot travel across the whole universe in one portal hop. We must use the existing folds in space.

I have neglected to ask you, Antura, whether it takes more than one portal jump to get from your planet to ours?

Yes. It takes two, although you thought it would only be one.

Are you able to use the same portals back to your planet, or are they just for one-way travel?

No, they are used in both directions. And to answer your next question, there is no danger of two spacecraft crashing in the middle of a portal hop. We have instruments that prevent such a collision.

Antura, are there one or more portals from Earth to the Moon, or is the distance too short to use a portal?

No, it is not too short. There are even waves or folds in space that can be used to make the trip instantaneously. But certainly we have the speed in these craft to make the trip in normal space in a very short period of time. You do have portals to all the planets in your solar system that you will be able to use one day.

Antura, the soul of the Moon told me I would be visiting her one day. I assumed it would be with you, so my question is, will we travel through a portal or simply at a fast rate?

We can do it either way. Perhaps we will go the slower, conventional way, and then on the way back, we will demonstrate a portal hop for you.

That would be a good idea. Perhaps we both landed on that idea at the same time, as I had not thought that before I asked.

Yes, I passed the idea along to you while you were typing the question.

Antura, when you portal hop to Earth, how do you know in which time period you will arrive?

We have instruments that zero in not only on the time but also which parallel life we wish to visit. These are simply frequencies, I shall call them for your purposes, so we naturally have known them for millions of years. It sounds complicated — and it is complicated to, say, an Earth human — but is not complicated for the technicians on board the spacecraft who may have dialed in the same time period hundreds of times.

Can you more fully describe these folds in space?

Oh, here we get into an area where I cannot give you too much information, as your scientists must discover this in the future.

Not even a simple explanation as you would give to a child?

No. The most I can say is they are like the appearance of waves in the ocean.

Before the number of questions I have today, I was viewing some images of distant galaxies taken by our Hubble telescope. They were gorgeous, but that reminded me to ask how you travel from this galaxy to another. How do you know which portal to take?

Now, that is a deep question. We have sensitive instruments, you see, that are far beyond your knowledge and capabilities. You understand that we can — to give you a simple explanation — enter the coordinates of the galaxy, and when we enter the portal, we wind up in that galaxy. From there, we can enter coordinates of whatever solar system and planet we wish to visit. Keep in mind that we probably already know where we're going, as we have perhaps already had visitors from that galaxy. There is much exploring done. You will do the same someday, and I'm speaking of Earth people in general.

Antura, when you go through a portal, do you see anything, such as a change in the color spectrum, bright colors, or just blackness?

Good question. Yes, we are able to see a quick burst of light as we move through the portal, but it is quite fast, as I have mentioned before that moving from one end of the portal to the other only takes a split second. It is not some lengthy movement from point A to point B.

So there are no colors?

No, just the burst of light.

Some time ago, you said that some galaxies were part of other universes, or did I receive that incorrectly?

No. What you see are galaxies in this universe, but certainly if you look far enough, you can glimpse other universes. I realize this sounds cryptic, but universes are not separated by enormous distances between them. You might say they are kissing cousins. It is expected that there should and will be interaction. As I have said before, there are even universes much larger than this one, and certainly universes tremendously smaller too. We all like to compare notes, you might say, at times.

You said there is an Earth portal to another universe. Is that correct?

Quite so. Keep in mind that I have also previously stated that you cannot go all the way across this universe without portal-hopping. That should tell you that the universe your portal goes to is not so far away.

CHAPTER 17

ATLANTIS

I had previously been told by my guardian angel that I had incarnated on the continent of Atlantis over 180 times during a period of 50,000 to 60,000 years. I have asked many questions about Atlantis that I'll publish in a future book, or you can go to my website, www.ETConversations.com, and read my archived weekly newsletters. The subject of Atlantis arose one day when I queried Antura as to the last life we spent together on Earth.

This was the life where I was inspired to create the Gentle Way of requesting benevolent outcomes. That time period was 200 years before Atlantis completely sank into the Atlantic Ocean, but the two warring factions were at each other's throats until the bitter end. So along with several thousand of the more than one million people using this simple spiritual tool, I packed up and emigrated through what is now Portugal and Spain and into a verdant Egypt. This was over 12,000 years ago.

Antura, when was the last Earth life we had together?

Long ago. Yes, all the way back to Atlantis. I have had other Earth lives since, just not together with you.

Requesting most benevolent outcomes (MBOs) is only necessary on Earth, isn't it?

Yes, you are the only people in the universe who are veiled, so this special spiritual tool is wonderful for you to use. It was a great inspiration when you received the information originally in Atlantis.

Were you with me in that life when I was inspired to create the Gentle Way?

Exactly. I was one of your best friends and assisted you in the move to Egypt. There was much to accomplish, and I worked with you to help resettle the multitude. I was a good tour guide, you might say.

When the experiment that resulted in what are termed the "things" by the Atlanteans, why didn't the ET society correct their mistake, or didn't some other society, such as the Pleiadians or Sirians, do it?

It's quite complicated. It was that society's experiment, and at that time, there was free reign to try any and all types of bodies to seek the perfect one for the Earth human. This one was allowed to go its course, as it came at the same time period the Adam man and woman were being introduced to the Atlantean continent. As you know, the Adam man and woman prevailed, and the societies involved sat back to see how they would handle the problem. It took the Atlanteans several thousand years to correct the genetic abnormalities. It was felt they should have this as part of their challenges.

Antura, what purpose did the artificial moon serve for the Atlanteans?

It served to transmit the crystal energy along with communications. And naturally, it lit up the sky to provide more light when the real moon was nearing its new moon phase. It existed for several thousand years before it was destroyed.

Going over the details just a little more, did the pieces of the artificial moon mostly fall onto the lands and seas of the world, or did parts of it wind up crashing into the Moon?

Yes, the explosion caused much of it to plunge into the ocean, but parts of it did crash into the Moon. And parts of it remained in orbit for quite a long time until they drifted and burned up in the atmosphere. It did cause a major rift in the relationship with the Arcturians, who constructed it.

Moving to Egypt

How many people immigrated with us from Atlantis to Egypt — a few hundred or a few thousand?

There were several thousand people who immigrated with us at that time. Certainly, it was way less than, say, even 10 percent of the people who were practicing or using benevolent outcome requests in their lives. Many could not leave families and had to stay behind. They lived out their lives on Atlantis before it actually sank into the sea. Their grandchildren's children were not so fortunate. Yes, that was down the line, as we moved some 200 years before Atlantis actually finally sank.

Were there Earth tremors all the time, say, similar to what Japan and New Zealand experience now?

Yes, and even worse. There were constant movements. It was a daily occurrence that everyone just learned to live with, but Gaia gave ample warning that that continent was not safe — keep in mind that parts of it had already sunk into the ocean — so the residents understood quite well what could happen at any time. Yet they continued their fighting and warring with each other right up until the end.

How much were we able to take with us?

It was not like we had a bunch of moving vans to transport all our possessions. Everyone was limited to what could easily be carried by hand and small wheeled carriers — slightly similar to those wheeled racks you have to carry luggage today but different. So everyone moved with virtually just the clothes on our backs, to use a popular phrase of today.

Was Egypt a tropical environment when we arrived?

Quite so. The desert expanded gradually over several thousand years.

When we arrived in Egypt from Atlantis, were the Sirian water people mentioned in Lois J. Wetzel's book Akashic Records *there already, or did they arrive later?*

Good question. Yes, they had recently arrived, knowing you and I would be arriving ourselves, you see. So there was an immediate connection.

Were the Sirians in ancient Egypt described in her book from your planet or another in your star system?

Good question. No, they were some of our forefathers, I shall call them.

But their appearance was described as looking like men from the waist up and fish from the waist down.

Yes, they took on that appearance for various reasons. But I can assure you that my appearance and that of my counterparts is very close to the descriptions I have given you in response to the questions you have previously asked.

Why were they there at that time?

They were there to assist the many refugees from Atlantis, along with the folk who were the original inhabitants of Egypt. But then the Federation Directive came down, and they had to abandon their small colony. As you read, they were already causing a problem because people from another country were trying to infiltrate the caretakers so that they could either undermine our efforts or use whatever information was being passed on to their own advantage.

Then it was not you and I that returned to Egypt after our Atlantean/Egyptian lives. Am I correct here?

Quite correct. These Sirian beings were people with functions not too different than mine, but they acted more as contact people for governments.

CHAPTER 18

ET CONTACTS

Antura, can you tell me what really happened at Roswell, New Mexico, back in 1947?

There was a crash of a scout craft from one of the worlds studying you. There was a loss of life, and the beings who died were studied by your scientists, who were sworn to secrecy, as there was great fear that your population would become very fearful and imagine an alien behind every tree. Therefore, your government created plausible or semi-plausible explanations in order to keep your citizens calm.

As has been reported, fear that humans might not be the smartest beings in the universe — or that there were beings capable of interstellar flight while all you had achieved was propeller aircraft along with the very beginning of jet power — would have led to great fear. Since you are veiled and cannot see your true magnificence, you have to feel you are at the top of the heap, so to speak, and that you are the smartest beings on your planet or any other.

In some ways, this is true or will be true as you go out to the stars and cause whole civilizations to begin growing again after being stagnant for thousands of years. But introducing ourselves so that there is not mass panic has been quite a difficult achievement. Again, you are rising in your knowledge and acceptance of beings different from you, thanks to all the science-fiction movies and the many sightings of our aircraft seen in your skies.

So Roswell was the first, but there have been a small number of other accidents or encounters during which an ET was injured or killed. These will come out in the future, much more so after the Pleiadians make their appearance in 2015, and more will be revealed.

Antura, did U.S. President Eisenhower meet with a delegation of ETs in the 1950s?

Quite so; this has become almost common knowledge.

Were they from the Pleiades?

Not exactly, but they certainly were similar in appearance to Earth humans so that there would be no fear. They met and it was agreed that the ETs would hold off from making public contact, as it was felt there would be much fear.

The Obama Inauguration

Was it a Federation spacecraft, or more than one, that buzzed the inauguration of President Barack Obama on January 20, 2009, an event that was captured on TV?

Quite so — there was more than one taking readings of that huge crowd of people. There are very few times when such masses of people are in one place, which enables these ships to compile massive amounts of data quickly.

Yes, but at the same time, they knew that there would be a million cameras — and I'm not exaggerating too much — recording the event, so they knew they would be seen.

Correct. That's part of their mission or goal — to let everyone know that they were there observing. Thousands, if not hundreds of thousands of people, will view these pictures and wonder who was in that ship.

How fast were they traveling, as they went through the whole frame of the TV screen image in seemingly half a second?

Correct. They did not have to hover nor could they, as there would have been a problem with your military aircraft had they done so. They sped through the area at easily over 2,000 miles per hour, fast enough so military craft could not or would not have been able to follow. It was even caught on their radar screens, but naturally this has been kept as classified information up to this point.

The spacecraft that was seen seemed to flap wings.

Yes, it had that appearance, but those wings, as they were called, were rapidly taking readings over a wide area, and no, they were not part of a propulsion system.

Then it was not a bird as someone claimed?

Certainly not. As you thought, it would have been an enormous bird to have been captured on video at that distance. And its speed was far beyond any bird's capabilities.

Do your spacecraft have the ability to measure compassion, anxiety, love, and vibrational levels?

Yes, would be the answer for all four. Again, we've been doing this for millions of years, so those feelings are all part of your etheric field around your bodies.

Have I left out anything else you measure in our etheric field?

Yes, but you will have to ask me. I can't volunteer the answer.

So I could add in happiness, sadness, and anger to those measurements?

Exactly. All human emotion would be the more general way to cover it. And not just emotions for humans — it can measure these emotions for all beings.

Were they only able to measure the group emotions in general, or were they able to take simultaneous readings of one million people?

No, these machines or computers — using your descriptive words — are capable of measuring that many individuals at one time. Not just the group as a whole, but certainly we can do that too.

So the mission was to gather data while being captured on film or tape, right?

Quite so. And I might add before you ask, the readings they obtained were very favorable to your development. A great sense of benevolence was observed in our readings.

The Sirians Were Earth Humans' First Protectors

{Author's Note: For those of you who have never heard of Nibiru, it is reported to be a planet that intersects with our solar system every 3,600 years or so on an elliptical orbit. It is also known as the twelfth planet. Zacharia Sitchin published several book about the planet and its rulers, which he had translated from Sumerian writings (Earth Chronicles series)].

Antura, is it true there were mines — gold mines — established by the rulers of the planet Nibiru at some point in our history?

Yes, this was very early in your history. But they did operate these mines using humans as laborers. And yes, they did fight among themselves for control of these mines.

Is it true that the Sirians were our first protectors?

Quite true. It was seen that you were being taken advantage of by interlopers, shall we call them, and we came and announced these activities would cease. So then you were left to grow mostly on your own but still with a lot of visits from us and others.

Who were the interlopers, as you called them, who were interfering with us when you became our protectors?

As you guessed, it was the Nibiruans. They were having a field day, as they were using Earth people as virtual slaves to do their mining and other work. The earthlings had no chance, as the Nibiruans had thousands of years to prepare to use Earth. They were forced to back off when we came and warned them to cease their operations.

Was this well before you interfered in Atlantis?

Yes, quite a few thousand years even before Atlantis, which is why you only have the ancient writings of the Sumerians.

Do you consider gold, silver, and diamonds to be valuable?

Certainly not in the same way you do, but yes, they have uses beyond just being pretty to look at. You'll find many more ways these metals and gems are used in the coming years.

Did your planet have anything to do with activating the crystal in Arkansas that some-one channeled about?

No, that was not our planet. As I mentioned before, there are over 200 planets, so in this case, it was someone else from the Federation.

Atlanteans

Antura, let's go back to ancient times. How many times did the mothership you will be arriving in travel to the continent of Atlantis, and were they always aware of its presence, never aware, or what? And how common was the contact?

Yes, the mothership traveled many times to Earth during that period of time, but it never came down and landed, shall we say. It was much easier to deploy the scout craft and either land and visit whoever they wished or take certain individuals in these craft back to the mothership.

Then was this the period of time that Master Kirael[5] spoke of when the Sirians were interfering when they shouldn't have been?

Yes, it would now be considered interfering. We assumed — and I should say wrongly assumed — that the Atlanteans were close to making the jump, as you are now. But as your guardian angel has told you before, greed collapsed their society into violence. We learned our lesson then.

It is my understanding that the Atlanteans were limited to suborbital flights due to the limits of the crystals. Is that correct?

Yes, exactly. They had to have those beams of energy created by the crystals for their flying machines. They were not internal but external sources of power. So the beams had a certain range that limited their flights to the suborbital variety, as you call it.

Ancient Egypt

Who built the pyramids of Giza?

That is the age-old question, is it not? Certainly the pyramids were built by humans but with the technical assistance, or rather advice, of your friendly ETs. It was naturally known that these structures would last for thousands of years and would create mysteries for those who would ponder your existence and where you came from. You must have mysteries, as you are so veiled.

Previous civilizations are covered up literally by the sands of time, as is shown to your archeologists over and over again when they must dig deep into the earth or sand as they discover these previous civilizations. As the Federation of Planets, we have been with you from the very start millions of years ago — not just a few thousand as some of your religions proclaim. As your guardian angel has told you before, Egypt was inhabited over 500,000 years ago, but the archeologists in Egypt cannot state these facts or they would be in danger of being hurt or slain due to the fundamentalist religion prevalent there.

Are there pyramids on other planets, or are they unique to Earth?

No, they are not unique to Earth. There are thousands of planets across the universe that have pyramids. You just have not discovered their use yet — at least not the scientific sector. This will soon be explained to you during the series of first contacts, along with an explanation of how they were built.

Someone asked if the pyramids, Mayan temples, and Stonehenge are all of human construction?

Yes, with a little assistance from your friendly ETs. We did not build them for you but gave technical assistance.

---

5   Master Kirael is a spirit guide from the seventh dimension (www.kirael.com).

When did the "gods" seemingly leave several thousands of years ago? If they were ETs, then where did they come from, and did they really leave or was that a perception?

It was no perception. They did leave, but this happened many thousands of years earlier than is reported. That's why there are legends that abound. They left due to the Earth Directive, which was strengthened after the Grays began kidnapping people. There were a variety of reasons for this, as they were meddling too much in your affairs. You might say that they were forced off. Your Sirian protectors were part of this effort.

Other Ancient Contacts

Who helped build the ancient city of Puma Punka?

As you were told by your guardian angel, it was built even before most of Atlantis. It was one of those experiments that did not last. This was not one of your "usual suspects," as you might call us. Again, it did not work out.

What about the Nazca lines in Peru? Were they ETs or locals?

Locals. Again, they had certain ceremonies and rituals and customs brought about through their contact with extraterrestrials long, long ago. It was another way to create a mystery — why would they make such lines that could only be seen from the air? They wanted these lines or images to be seen from heaven.

It has made you wonder to this day and contemplate the mystery so that on a subconscious or subliminal level, you would understand that we have been in contact with you for thousands of years — way past your recorded time.

Antura, who built the Bosnian Pyramid complex located near Sarajevo, and were there ETs involved?

Certainly there were ET advisors, as this was and is a very important pyramid complex. As has been discovered, there is a beam of energy that goes out across the universe, and you will discover the reason why this is in not too long a time when the Pleiadians begin their visits. The concrete used to form the slabs covering the pyramids is of better quality than the concrete manufactured today, plus there are tunnels and rooms used for healing beneath the complex.

Therefore, the people who constructed the complex were well assisted by their ET brothers. They constructed this complex for their religious ceremonies and practices and were told these structures would last many thousands of years.

Were the people who constructed these complexes from Atlantis, since there is carbon dating pointing to a time 26,000 years ago?

No, these people were not Atlanteans. The Atlanteans gave them a wide berth, you might say, as they were protected by their ET friends. They had a duty to create these structures, knowing their use, and felt quite honored to be chosen to create them. Later they would have to be sealed up to protect them from marauding bands of warriors. This was done more than once during their existence. Now they will be slowly uncovered so that many tourists and scientists can enjoy their beauty once again.[6]

What is your explanation of the underground cities in Brazil?

Certainly the Federation has had some there in the past, as it was pretty remote and various readings and tests were easy to take there. This is not the case now, but some will be pointed out to people in the future.

Why did ETs construct Lake Titicaca in the Andes on the border of Peru and Bolivia?

It was a major base quite a few thousand years ago. This was even before the time of Atlantis, so we are talking about ancient history. But as things happened during that time, they basically reduced its use. It is still used today but to a much lesser extent, simply for research. It would be as if you took over an old building that needed repairs and fixed it up and remodeled it.

Dreams

Is there is a way to visit Federation ships during our sleep or dream time?

Yes, but it requires dreamers to be able to dream lucidly and request that they be accompanied to a Federation ship that would receive them. Naturally, it would be best if they visit a ship from their own star system or home planet. As has been reported, some people are taken there by their own people and introduced to concepts and to the ship itself to prepare them for when the Federation ships come to visit publicly. There will be much more of this during the years leading up to public contact so that the fear level of the population as a whole will not be so high.

How do you manipulate us in our dream time to visit the ships?

This is fairly easy to do from our point of view. In future years, you will learn much about the etheric body and eventually how to control it yourselves. This is not too far in your future, but it is far enough that it sounds like science fiction at this time. We are simply able to project ourselves — naturally, with the soul's permission — to take the place of what you call your "dream angels" and escort you to the spaceships. It is all done in a meditative state. We do not use fancy instruments or machines. Our training allows us to meet you on a dream level. You may also notice from reading about other close encounters that it seems like a dream to these people, as it is difficult to recall. This is all accomplished, as I said before, with your soul's permission for your learning purposes.

How are souls manipulated into spaceships even though they agree on a soul level?

This is a sophisticated maneuver, which again, is far ahead of you in time. Once you go out to the stars yourself, you'll see this in action with various societies. The souls are not only guided by their dream angels, as you call them, but by people on the ship in a meditative state, shall we call it. It can be an almost instantaneous process to move them to the ship and be able to work on their esoteric bodies, shall we call them. But again, keep in mind that this is with their souls' full approval, or it would not be done.

Why did I have a dream about little four-foot tall androids?

You were actually visiting a world where androids are being introduced now. You were experiencing the conflict of emotions people had in accepting these androids.

Are these androids capable of having children?

Yes, in this case, they do have the ability to conceive. It's less costly than having facilities to turn them out one by one.

Modern Day Contacts

Antura, can you tell me anything additional about the Rendlesham Forest Incident[7] of 1980? Who was there?

They were Federation scout ships — or just one such ship, I should say. It was another instance when we knew the story would not or could not be buried by the government. And it remains to be told over thirty years later.

Do the creators, shall we call them, of various Earth races such as the Dogon people and the Aborigines visit them?

Yes, they actually do visit them on occasion. They visit only the elders, who are schooled in the old stories and have been in contact with them for thousands of years.

Do they remember these contacts?

Oh yes, we do not do it during sleep time but as actual physical contact. Naturally we — meaning the Sirians — take on an appearance just like these people in order to not frighten them, as they are humans and their creators do not look exactly the same. And they cherish their experiences.

Are the Aborigines leaving Earth as has been reported by at least one channel?

No, not to the extent they say. The Aborigines are here for the change, just as all people on Earth are. They will move into the fifth dimension just as you will in a short time.

What information can you give me on the Russian Kirsan Ilyumzhinov[8] who claims to have been abducted?

That did happen to this person during those times before such practices were stopped.

Please explain more about the abductions of people from Earth by your people. I thought these abductions were done primarily by the Grays, as we call them.

Yes, that is correct. Our abductions were much gentler and mainly involved passing along information to certain scientists and such that we were allowed to communicate with on a soul level. The Grays were desperate to avoid annihilation, so they were heavy-handed in their abductions. As I mentioned before, we corrected that.

Antura, are there black-eyed ET children asking for rides?

No. This is an old wives' tale in a way, but it also comes from memories of actual encounters. The memories fed to these people were of children, but of course they remembered the black eyes, which in real life are larger than the images they recall. Overall, these images were created when they abducted someone and took them back to their spacecraft so as not to frighten them. It was only partially successful.

I assume you are referring to the Zetas?

Quite so.

Do the Grays live beneath the surface in large numbers?

No, although their numbers were larger in the past. Now, just a few live beneath the surface.

Antura, are the Gray aliens the Zetas?

Correct.

Are most ETs from the present, Antura, or are there some from the past and future who contact us?

Almost all are from the present. The Federation curtailed most of the activities from your past.

What about the reported robotic-looking humanoids in India?

That's a different group, but the Federation allowed them to be there, as long as no humans were interfered with or contacted personally. I will add that there is great activity now that you are close to bridging over to the fifth focus. If there is any more traffic, we will have to have police directing the spaceships — that is a humorous comment.

Do beings from both the light and dark side live among us at the present time?

Certainly there are those with good intentions and a few with not so good intentions who live on the surface and attempt to sway you in one direction or another. They are quite limited, as they cannot use any supernatural powers or any instruments, devices, and so on.

A lady asked me about an alien being who appeared in her driveway and living room — this is an ET from where? Is there a connection with her husband? Was there a feud between two planets?

Yes, I will confirm that there were ETs, as you call them, in both places. They're from the couple's home planet, and they should have been a little more discreet, shall we say. Her husband is quite well known on his home planet, and there are those from elsewhere who might have wished him harm but were prevented from hurting him by his home people.

There was a feud going on between the two planets, which is finally being settled, and life will return back to normal for them. This is quite unusual, as there is peace between almost all the worlds these days. People were dispatched — you can call them ambassadors who have experience in settling disputes — similar to the people you have on Earth who do this work. They have brought the two sides together to resolve their differences.

UFO Sightings

Antura, why have so many ET craft or UFOs been seen around the Moon?

They were on various explorations. Plus they knew they would be seen, so it was a reminder to all who see the video footage.

---

7   Also known as Britain's Roswell, the Rendlesham Forest Incident is one of the best documented and most significant military-UFO encounters (www.theRendleshamForestIncident.com).

Is there a Moon base?

Yes, of a type, not anything major. It is just used for some studies and an easy way to keep hidden from Earth.

Would you please comment on the UFO sightings over Manhattan [October 2010, http://www.dailymail.co.uk/news/article-1320523/UFO-brings-streets-New-York-standstill.html] and China [August–October 2012] in recent times?

Yes. They were your friendly ETs reminding everyone that we are here. They were a little lonesome, shall we say, as they would be much happier doing a full visitation, but these flights are needed to keep up appearances. These two were from different places in the universe — yes, Andromeda is one of the places; no, the other one was not from Sirius, as you were thinking. This other one's home would be perhaps a little difficult to convey, as you don't know the area. Their job, as always, is to keep reminding you that there are other beings in the sky who mean you no harm.

May I remind everyone that you are quite safe and protected by order of the Federation. No more abduction for experiments is allowed, even though the ones that did happen were performed with the soul's consent. Being veiled, you did not know this, and they were frightening experiences for those taken away in the middle of the night.

These days all visiting species, shall we call ourselves, are only here to observe and give gentle reminders of our presence. Naturally, the governments still say we are weather balloons and other such tripe. They do have their reasons, as humans can be frightened by the appearance of a mouse, much less a large spacecraft. You have too many movies on wars of the worlds and invasions and such. Good theater, but not so good for preparations for our coming together, I assure you.

Was there any particular reason for a UFO to appear over the St. Petersburg airport in Russia [April 2012], and are Russians more accepting of UFOs than the citizens of the U.S.A.?

Good question. Yes, we did want it to be known that we — "we" meaning generally everyone — are here, so we put a spacecraft over an airport. With all of their radar and people watching the sky, it certainly makes the news, even all around the world. So yes, a Federation ship was there.

Regarding the Russian acceptance of extraterrestrial life, yes, a slightly higher percentage of people in Russia are more accepting than those in the United States. They are not brainwashed by their government, as are people in the United States, to believe these spacecraft are weather balloons and such nonsense.

Was there a spaceship over Denver on May 14, 2012?

Yes, this was a similar instance to the one where a Federation flew craft over St. Petersburg, Russia. Both sightings caused a lot of talk, which was what we wanted.

Another reported sighting was of the UFOs seen above Denver on several occasions recently. Were they friendly ETs or experimental spacecraft?

---

8   Former President of the Republic of Kalmykia in the Russian Federation from 1993 to 2010 and also the President of FIDE (World Chess Federation).

They were not experimental craft but friendly ETs. They were accomplishing two missions. They were making people notice them and doing some readings.

Was the UFO seen over Brooklyn, New York, on June 6, 2012, real or fake?

It was real. The pixilated image does reveal a spacecraft, although not one you normally see. This one was in the shape of a diamond or spinning top, if you prefer that description, and it was not a Federation ship. It was allowed to be there for studies. We also liked that it would be seen and discussed.

Is the news regarding the sightings of spacecraft making any headway with Earth people?

Yes. Again, these sightings are there as reminders. Slowly but surely, the population — especially the younger ones — are accepting that you are not the only living beings in all the billions of planets out there in all the billions of solar systems. Your religions downplay this or even reject the idea, thinking that you couldn't handle the truth. Slowly but surely, we are breaking down that wall of resistance and disbelief.

Antura, will there be any large UFO sightings coming up in the near future for largely populated areas?

Yes, as you have noticed, these sightings have become much more numerous, and certainly one of the reasons is that when it is summer, we know that people are more likely to be outside. So we — meaning the Federation in general — take advantage of the summertime with everyone out and about to put on displays, knowing that we are being photographed and recorded on video devices.

Just keep looking to the skies, folks — that would be my suggestion for anyone. Requesting MBOs to see a UFO, as you call the ships, will assist you in making that connection. Of course, those who wish for proof will have to carry a video recording device or camera with them at all times after making this MBO request.

What was the purpose of the spacecraft flying in and out of the sandstorm in Arizona on July 5, 2011, as seen on YouTube?

First, there's the obvious: The pilot of the spacecraft knew there was a helicopter with a video recording device flying in front of the sandstorm, so it was a perfect time to be seen flying around the sandstorm, in and out of it. Another reason for choosing that time is that it is quite known by pilots that you do not fly in and out of sandstorm, if they want their craft to remain in flight, as the sand will quickly clog up the engine, resulting in a crash landing. But these spacecraft do not have problems with sand, so it was a demonstration that this was not just some aircraft with a bright light flying in and out of the sandstorm. People would have to realize that the craft was something else. It is a little difficult for the government to claim it was a weather balloon or some light abnormality when the craft appeared at different heights and flew in and out of the cloud.

Again, this was a demonstration to be recorded. The spacecraft did not have the assignment of studying the sandstorm per se. Its mission was to be photographed, and yes, there was more than one of them. Yes, these were Federation spacecraft

— scout crafts — fairly small in comparison to, say, the one in which we will travel from the mothership to see you.

Jim, who is helping me on the book, received the following email from his friend Peggy in November 2012: "Strange observation at Vanderbilt Beach, Florida (near Naples), around 9:30PM. Over a half-hour period, I watched in amazement as four orange flying objects smoothly glided close overhead from east to west, disappearing in the clouds to the south of the crescent moon. They appeared one at a time about eight minutes apart and made no sound. Any thoughts what I could've been seeing? They almost looked like fireballs — very curious." What were they doing, Antura?

Yes, another set of readings were being taken. You are the most analyzed planet in the universe. These balls were placed there by another civilization that was not part of the Federation but was allowed to take readings, and they allowed themselves to be seen.

The Florida people would like to interact with those in the craft they saw near Naples, Florida, that I asked you about.

We are not allowed to interact under the directions of the Federation. This will change a little after the Pleiadians make first contact in 2015. Then the door will be slightly opened for other members of the Federation to send representatives, but again, it will be a slow process. Our visit there in 2017 will be one of the first allowed under the Directive. By then, there will be much information conveyed to your leaders and people about the history and workings of the Federation.

Is the YouTube video I saw of a UFO flying near Roswell, New Mexico, real or fake [view the video at http://www.youtube.com/watch?v=dh5xK5Emp6Q]?

Fake. They did a good job of combining it with footage actually shot in that area.

If you'll scan my memory bank, was the YouTube video I saw of a UFO landing in China real or computer-generated imagery (CGI)? [View the video at http://www.youtube.com/watch?v=X_aqyBNRgxU.]

Quite the latter, but it was very well done. It had just a couple of flaws here and there. We appreciate the attempt, as it makes people think and keeps us in the news, shall we say.

SETI, Crop Circles, and Phobos

Why don't the SETI (Search for Extraterrestrial Intelligence) receivers ever record ET transmissions?

Tom, we are millions of years ahead of you in technology. We have long since passed using the forms of communication you have now on Earth. There are much better ways to communicate, but it will take some years for these technologies to be rediscovered by Earth people. Right now, you would only have the opportunity to listen to a society that matches up almost exactly to your society's accomplishments. As you've learned from our conversations, there are many, many societies out there that have not reached your level of development, as well as societies that are far beyond yours. I will not call what the SETI people are doing a waste of time. Rather, I will just say that their efforts will result in discoveries other than that of life on other planets.

What can you tell me about how crop circles are created?

Yes, this has been recorded by those with cameras. There are small robotic craft with the simple job of causing the wheat in the fields to lay down in mathematical patterns. These are reminders, again, of our presence. Although officials have claimed these are just people creeping around creating these symbols in order to keep the population calm, there is sufficient evidence that these crop circle formations are created instantaneously — or at least in two- to five-minute periods — to shoot holes in these claims.

These symbols appeal to those with mathematical backgrounds, artists, and even regular people who see the beauty in these formations, even though they don't understand what the symbols mean. They are difficult even for someone versed in symbology and mathematics and geometry. They are done to motivate you to consider how they are formed and by whom.

Why are most of them in southern England, and can you say more about who creates them?

Yes, as everyone has noted, these crop circles can be considered massive works of art with geometric and mathematical themes. Southern England was chosen due to its lack of population, yet it has just enough people so that the symbols would be quickly found and photographed. The beings who do this are your friendly Arcturians, and they do this to create mysteries and yet also point out how they are crafted by intelligent species. They have no sinister motives; they are designed to make mathematicians, along with the general population, ponder their meanings.

They are created by small robotic craft that have been photographed as they create these crop circles. These symbols are used all over the universe, so they should be studied in more detail, as they are not just works of art. There are messages behind them that will slowly be discovered over time.

Is the Martian moon Phobos an artificial satellite?

Yes and no. Parts of it have been reshaped, and other remnants of the Martian society will be discovered. Ancient ruins exist that can be explored.

Who built it?

It was built in truly ancient times by the Martian people. There will be a wealth of information found on it, and it will be viewed as having had a lot of work done on it. The Earth explorers will hit the jackpot when they begin to visit this partly artificial moon. Much will be learned there.

Spiritual Connections

Was the mother of Jesus impregnated by an ET, and if so, by whom?

Not in the least. This was not done by any ET, unless you consider Jesus an ET. His soul was quite capable of having his future mother Mary be impregnated in advance of his birth, you see. There was no need for an ET to accomplish this.

Do ETs interact with the Elohim?

Yes, in the concept or basis in which this was asked. We are in constant contact with our spiritual advisors who are not in physical form. This is quite common elsewhere in the galaxy as compared to Earth, where you are veiled from knowing your true relationship to your souls and think you are all alone in the universe. This has been done, as has been explained to you before, for a purpose — so you will re-create all that has been done before but will find new ways of creating never before thought of by any other race. To answer the question again, yes, we are in touch with our spiritual advisers every day through meditation.

Antura, please explain who the Ashtar Command is.

Here we get into a rather sensitive area, as those who claim to be the Ashtar Command are souls who know their purpose, which is to give structure and a hierarchy system to those people who feel the need for such. When you bridge over to the fifth focus, your need for such structure will be slowly reduced. The channelings will become more accurate then.

Why can't RH negative blood be cloned? Was this from the original experiment or what?

RH negative blood is, in a way, the original blood used, but you do not know how it can be cloned or duplicated yet. It is a mystery to you and will cause your researchers to study the differences in its DNA makeup from that of other blood types.

Speculation

Antura, there is a lot of speculation about the United States or other countries and organizations having spacecraft. Is this true or not?

As has been previously told, these reports have been exaggerated. You do have some aircraft, we will call them, beyond what is admitted in the normal news, but these craft do not have the capability of flying to the Moon or Mars and so forth.

Naturally, the military has been financing these craft, but true interplanetary travel is still twenty-five to thirty years ahead for you. There is much development still to be done before that occurs. Don't forget that there are those who wish to make money who make wild claims with no basis in fact for their fifteen minutes of fame, as you call it; then they can earn fees from their books and speaking engagements. The more outlandish these claims sound, the more they attract attention.

I have been told that thirty or forty years ago, "friendly aircraft" — American, I believe — were flying over Russia and returning to Alaska at speeds up to 6,000 miles per hour. Your comments?

This is somewhat of an exaggeration. Yes, there were aircraft at that time that traveled up to 2,000 miles per hour but not as fast as your friend's friend reported. And certainly these aircraft were kept top secret both then and now. Of course, they were monitored by your friendly ETs, and certainly there were times that our ships were clocked in the speed range you mention. They were observing and taking notes, shall we say, of your aircraft performances and missions.

I saw a story on video a couple of days ago where a gentleman was claiming that there were top-secret U.S. aircraft capable of speeds of 12,000 miles per hour. Your comments?

Yes. These look good on paper, but your scientists have yet to be able to launch such vehicles. They're still in the drawing stages. We would know immediately if there was anyone flying around in one of these aircraft, especially when they could pose a danger to us. These drawings were made up, and dummy aircraft models were even used so that there wouldn't be fear. If these are top-secret, human-made aircraft, then no one will worry or ponder that there are actually intelligent beings out there. They'll just say, "Oh there's another of our aircraft," and although amazed at the speed, they will just think, "It's one of ours." Trust me on this one.

Antura, there are images I've seen purported to be of some type of object going through the meteor in the sky above Russia [February 2013, view the video at http://www.youtube.com/watch?v=UqJP3til0Ig]. Was this true or was it CGI? And if it was true, was it a Russian missile or an ET-controlled object that did not explode but simply broke apart the meteor?

In this case, it was decided that this errant meteor would cause severe destruction, so one of the Federation ships monitoring the meteor sent the equivalent of a missile with no explosive warhead to break apart the meteor before it could do real damage instead of just the sonic boom.

Why are there reports about some places suffering damage and a few yards away there was no damage?

When the meteor was broken apart, some shock waves traveled out in a narrow band, depending on the size of the projectiles. Other shock waves created the broad destruction of windows and structures that was reported.

We have heard stories of people killed and work destroyed by those who wish to keep free energy away from our use. Is this true? And if it is true, was this done by private companies or one or more governments?

Yes, this is a long-running conspiracy theory. Certainly there are some kernels of truth to the stories in which large oil companies have stepped in at times to buy off research in order to protect and extend the demand for oil. Money is a great motivator to someone who has lived quite some time on an academic salary, shall we way. The stories of deaths have been exaggerated. I will not say they have not happened, as I would need to scan a number of records, but I do know some buying off has occurred.

Creating the Explorer Race

How many species have contributed DNA to the Earth Experiment — over twenty?

Yes, more than twenty — certainly all of the species wanted to contribute, but it was found that there was a great overlapping. So there are not many more than twenty who contributed, as there were other species that were descendants, shall we say, of the contributing ones.

Is it true that the Lyrans wanted us to only have Simian eyes?

Quite true. They did not want you to appear like the majority of the universe. They wanted you to feel as if you were the only beings to exist in the universe each time you viewed yourselves in a mirror.

But was this partially because they wanted to be viewed as the top dogs?

Yes. Naturally, they were looking far down the road to the time when you would one day come calling.

Would you give me any information on the root languages on Earth and where they originated from?

I'll do my best.

Let's begin with Latin.

Yes, the Pleiades.

Chinese?

It's planetary system far off the beaten track, shall we say. Not one of the normal sun groups.

Arabic?

The Arcturians.

English?

More Pleiadian, but you understand this language is an amalgamation of several sources.

Antura, what Earth languages originated from the Sirius B or A system?

As you may have guessed, the Germanic languages originated in this star system.

Where did the Japanese language originate?

Not in this system. It is a system you're not familiar with, but it is obviously part of the Federation.

So Nibiru had no part in providing this or other languages?

No, but they influenced them, shall we say, during the time they were close by due to their orbit. Keep in mind that each language certainly originated over a million years ago in Earth time.

So let's go back to your star system for a minute. Did all the Germanic languages originate in the Sirius B system or did some come from the Sirius A system?

There you have it. Both star systems created these languages, as they have worked together for literally billions of years.

When you use those numbers, Antura, it really amazes me — first, by how young our society is here on Earth, and second, by how far you have come yet how far you still need to go in raising your vibrational levels. That is, if the 5.3 to 5.4 level you said is correct for all the universe. Or should I limit that to the Federation planets or even to certain star systems?

No, you would be accurate in using those figures for the whole universe, at least for the fifth focus. Keep in mind that there are even higher focuses we work with such as the seventh focus, but the planetary societies are mired at this level in the fifth focus. As I have stated before, we look toward the Explorer Race's arrival with great anticipation but certainly with some trepidation as well, as we know our societies will forever change. We realize that this is for our own good, but as you know, what you have become used to over millions of years feels comfortable. To change something you are so used to feels as if you are about to step out into space, trusting that there is an invisible walkway. Yes, this analogy is similar to a scene from *Indiana Jones and the Last Crusade*.

Why Observe Us?

Has there been anything that your observers have noted lately regarding Earth that you found interesting?

Yes, we see a great deal of Earth movements, and our readings indicate that you are expanding in not only your vibrational level but also in your knowledge. That is what has impressed us the most. We took hundreds of thousands of years to do what you are doing in only a few thousand — very impressive, but we knew that going in.

Would you please explain why we are the most observed planet in the universe, and could we go one, two, three?

1. You have, as a planetary society, been the only ones to work with negativity and to do so successfully in the history of the universe.
2. You are the only society to be veiled from knowing your connection with your souls and your past lives.
3. You are the only society to have a time loop in which you are experiencing all of your lives at the same time.
4. You will be the only society that ever transfers from one focus to the next while everyone on the planet is alive.

Can you explain negativity?

Yes, I'll try. Negativity is a force or energy, just as positive energy is; it is simply the opposite energy. But it has been impossible to work with or in, so all other societies shoved it under the rug, shall we say. The purpose of the Earth Experiment was to see whether somehow a society could learn to work and even thrive in extreme negativity, which the Earth society has been able to do as a whole.

Now the amount of this negative energy you work with will slowly ebb over the next one hundred years, let's say, since you were successful. You are the first society in this universe or any other universe to successfully work with it without blowing yourselves up. This is a tremendous accomplishment, and everyone is amazed at your success. This is why, as I have said previously, "parking is at a premium," because spaceships from all over this universe — and yes, even spaceships from other universes — are taking these very intricate readings of things your scientists would know nothing of to study.

What types of negativity will we introduce to other societies, and how can we cover everyone?

It seems like a formidable task — perhaps even impossible. But once you begin to introduce simple things like games that require winners and losers, they will spread — variations of these, you understand — to many other societies across the universe. We are fortunate in this Federation to be the first to receive this small negativity to work with, although we are a little anxious, because these societies have been around for millions of years, so any change will be enormous for us.

It is my understanding that there is nowhere else in the universe with negativity?

Quite so — not even the reptilians.

What about the society living on Earth on the lower third-dimensional rungs, shall we say, that is living with negativity? [This society was discussed briefly in chapter 11.]

I stand corrected, and yes, there is even another world being set up to have negativity like Earth but in a much lower amount.

Time Travel

Antura, is time travel only possible in the Earth time loop, or can anyone in the universe travel back and forth in time?

Excellent question. No, time travel is only available in this time loop. This is why we can, should we desire, meet and converse with societies from the past and future. This is quite complicated, but the very nature of your time loop allows societies from any time in the past to access the different time periods. Finally, the Federation Directive has regulated and actually restricted this, so it was much more prevalent in the past — your past — than in your present.

Do you — meaning other societies — harmonize with a specific frequency signature to time travel?

Yes, in a way. Certainly there is a tuning in to the frequency signature of a specific time period. This is so advanced that you will not learn about it yourselves until very far in the future, as you can imagine.

Okay, but am I to understand that time travel is not done in the rest of the universe?

Yes, that is correct. It is only done in special time continuums.

Disclosures

Antura, will there be any disclosures around June 21 of this year [2011]?

No. The European country that will be making disclosures will not do this for a couple of more years, I can assure you. But I can also assure you that when it happens, there will be a great tumultuous outcry, as there are those who wish to keep this information secret in the belief that "you can't handle the truth," as that actor in that movie said. But it will open the door so that, as more countries open up their previously secret archives, it will become widespread knowledge.

When will the European country have disclosure?

Not for another two years, as you guessed. The time is not right yet, and when 2012 comes along, there will be the great shift. There will also be a great shift in people's attitudes and desire for more information and disclosure as we move toward that point.

CHAPTER 19

CONTACTING OTHER PLANETS

Antura, how is contact made with other planets?

Good question. Normally, we seek out the leaders of a planet after careful study from afar, or at least from where they are not able to see us and become concerned. This might also be a joint mission with beings from other planets, as we work closely with a number of other planets or societies in this Federation of Planets of which we're a member.

People are chosen that would most relate to the society we want to contact to introduce ourselves. That way, there is no concern from those we contact that we are there for anything but a peaceful, fruitful contact in which we can offer them things that can be used by a society less developed than our own.

Naturally, this is done when we feel they have reached the stage at which we can contact them and it will be beneficial for all parties. Of course, it will happen soon, and you'll get to see the process firsthand.

When you visit a new planet, is there a set of guidelines you follow? And if that is the case, can you give me some examples?

Yes, certainly guidelines have been used for thousands, if not millions, of years. That would include not providing the society with any weapons or high-tech devices until such time as any of them would be welcomed. We are to honor their choices of life, whatever that may be. We are to offer our assistance in the future, depending on their level of development. The bottom line is that we say we're available should they have any problems they can't solve.

I would think it would be quite different for Earth?

You're quite right there. We had to write a completely different set of rules to accommodate your unique circumstances. All the other rules had to be examined one by one and new ones designed for you. It did take time and effort, but those were incorporated in the Earth Directive.

Do you have a favorite planet in the universe that you like to visit other than Earth?

Yes. Naturally, it is another water planet, which would not be too hard to guess. It's a lovely planet in a far-off system with many unique inhabitants and beautiful underwater flora and formations. It's a very pleasant planet to swim in, as you can imagine.

What about a least favorite planet to visit?

Yes, there are several. Certainly, a planet with little or no water and very harsh surface conditions is not my cup of tea. We are easily able to visit these planets and survive even the harshest conditions with the spacecraft and our devices that put invisible shields around us. But those visits are short or as at least brief as possible, depending on what our mission is for that planet.

What galaxy in this universe have you visited that was most interesting to you?

The Sombrero Galaxy is one that was very interesting with a large variety of beings. Each galaxy and each universe has its own differences, so when you visit each one, each has its own flavor, if you will.

The Desert Planet

What type of world was the last one you visited as a first contact?

It was a pleasant planet, but quite different from Earth. It was a very dry, desert-type planet, and the beings were, shall we say, quite different from humanoids. They were coming to the point in their evolution at which we could introduce ourselves, but would still be considered much younger, shall we say, than Earth residents.

Remember, we've been in contact with Earth beings of all different types for hundreds of thousands of years. So we generally start at an earlier development stage than it would seem from your perspective.

Were you part of a delegation or an individual contact?

Both. We like to make individual contacts, along with the more group-oriented or government contacts. It will vary depending on what the form of life might be; there are so many differences in this regard that it would be impossible to explain to you at this stage, but we'll work on that in the future.

What is your specialty in these contacts?

Ah, after 800 lives on Earth, I do have the gift of gab, so to speak, or an ability to work with a large number of different beings. And those Earth lives gave me the ability to make these contacts work and to solve any problems that arise.

How was the desert planet discovered?

It was one of our scout ships. I say one of ours, because in actuality it was a Federation scout ship that was taking readings of a star system and found that there was life on several planets, including the desert planet.

How many Earth years ago was that?

Not so many — certainly less than a couple of hundred Earth years.

How long did you study the planet before making contact?

Certainly it was less than 200 Earth years. We have very detailed instruments that measure things you've never considered, plus all the normal things you would imagine to be useful in studying a new planet. It's just that this is done quite quickly, as again we have developed instruments over thousands and thousands of years to quickly do these studies and assimilate them with what you term computers.

Did they have anything to offer or barter?

Not really at this time. We made the contact as a goodwill gesture, you could call it, and we will offer them some assistance in the future.

What did the beings on that desert planet you contacted look like? Were they humanoid?

No, they were not. They would be a little difficult to describe, but certainly they have the appearance of a sloth, although much larger. And yes, they do burrow in the sand, but they are intelligent and will accomplish much in the coming years.

Then they do not have cities or villages?

Quite so. I know you might think that we would only contact much more advanced civilizations, but again, we contact beings on planets thousands of years before they make that jump. That's why we only needed a short time to study them, as they are still a very basic form of life but intelligent. Our instruments are able to read that intelligence and determine that they will progress to eventually have a thriving society.

Is there a common method of defining intelligence in Federation protocol when you do a first contact?

Yes, I suppose you could say so. We hearken back to those measurements, which can also measure the intelligence of the beings on a planet we are studying. It is quite easy to measure the IQ, using Earth terms, of all the beings on a given planet to know which category to place a particular species in. You are just in the beginning stages of doing this, and I can tell you that your scientists have a *long* way to go to learn how to measure intelligence.

Did you have to disguise yourselves in order to communicate with them and not frighten them?

Yes, actually we did. That's something we have not gotten into yet. We are able to take on a form, if needed, so that the beings we contact are not frightened out of their wits, to use your vernacular.

Then you take these forms that must be holographic — or are they?

Yes, there you have it. We project an advanced, holographic image to them that looks and feels like the real thing. Again, we do this to keep from frightening beings who have not even considered the possibility of beings who look different from what they are familiar with on their world.

Then did you appear as a giant sloth, or did you appear as some other non-threatening creature?

In that case, we appeared rather similar to the sloth beings, shall we call them, but certainly a non-aggressive sort of sloth. Yet we had the appearance of age and knowledge — what they perceived as wise, older sloths to them.

When you make first contacts with other planets, Antura, are they all in the fifth focus, third focus, a mixture, or do you study them in different focuses?

Very good question. Certainly, we have the ability to switch focuses at will and do so when we are contacting a planet for the first time. That way, we can study them completely. So to answer the question, we do make complete studies of a planet through which we discover life on it through all its focuses — yes, even higher than the fifth.

Work on Other Planets

Can you expand on your job or work some more? How many planets have you visited as part of your work, aside from pleasure trips?

Several.

More than ten?

Yes, but just barely above that number. Let's say twelve for your purposes.

That's not very many considering your age, is it?

No, but again we visit these worlds, stay for some time gathering information, and in my case, making contact, and then we return while others take our places — if more time is needed to study the cultures on a planet.

Then besides the desert planet, what other types of planets have you visited?

There have been a couple of gaseous-type planets whose societies we studied lived beneath the surface, some in various forms of liquid, including my own planet's specialty water. That's another thing to keep in mind — we Sirians are brought in if there are water planets discovered, as we can easily handle those environments to seek out the various varieties of fish and other forms of life that make oceans their home. And some of these societies are quite complex.

What is the most unusual intelligent being you've met during your travels?

Oh, where to start! That's a difficult question, but there are some enormous beings, shall we call them, who are part of the landscape of a world. That was pretty unusual. There are so many others; we can cover more of them at a later time.

How long ago were you involved in the first contact of a water world, and how far along the path, shall we say, was their development?

Just a few years ago in universal time. The world we visited is still in an early stage of development; as I explained, there are many worlds just like these that you will encounter when you travel to the stars.

So we introduced ourselves, and naturally, we appeared to them as they looked so as not to frighten them. They have many thousands of years of development ahead of them before they are ready to travel even to other planets in their own solar system. But again, that's our job — to make these contacts and then return periodically to check on their progress.

Are you familiar with the amphibians who live in a world where the oceans are completely different from water, beings who are able to propel themselves through the water at speeds of 300 miles per hour or so?

Quite so, and no, they are not us. They are another amphibian race who, naturally, we know intimately — another version of the same type of being. And yes, they are quite fast in the liquid they inhabit.

Are they in the Sirius star system or another?

No, they are in another galaxy.

Do you assist other societies in your dream state as earthlings do?

No, not in the same way, as we are not veiled as you are. That's why you cannot remember many of your dreams, as you would learn too much about your capabilities and who you really are. No, I am asked on occasion to consult with a society, but there are billions of Earth soul fragments on hand each night to do this work, so we are not called on anywhere near to the extent you are.

How far in advance are our dream sojourns planned?

Weeks in advance. As I mentioned before, you are quite in demand to assist other societies in the universe to assist them with their problems. Even people with just a few Earth lives can solve many questions and problems, but people like you personally — with many Earth lives under your belt, shall we say — are in high demand, so everyone has to take the proverbial number and await their turn.

Besides "good life," what other interstellar greetings do you have?

Greetings such as "may the Creator bring you happiness and a long life." Some of the greetings are fairly formal, as you might imagine, for occasions in which we are doing business or having some type of political or Federation business in which we do not know the beings personally but are there to discuss common interests.

Beings of the Universe

Are you familiar with the bird people of Eaglelia?

Yes, quite so. They are beautiful people, as has been reported.

It is my understanding that you are focused in the fifth dimension, so are they too?

Quite so. And yes, the bird men of Eaglelia are focused both in the fifth dimension and in the seventh. This is all very complicated for you and people in general at this time, but in the coming years, you will learn more about these dimensional focuses.

Are the cyclops race we discussed before larger, the same size, or smaller in statue than a normal earthling?

Good question. They do have several different sizes, as you can imagine, because this race is present on different worlds and Creator likes variety. There are some much larger than you — almost twice your size — and there are some petite one-eyed beings only a little larger than half your size. And there are some who are the same size as you. So there is no one answer to that question, as there are millions of varieties of humanoids, as you will come to learn in the coming years.

Who is the largest humanoid you have ever encountered?

One race of cyclops measures around fifteen feet (four-and-a-half meters) in height. But there are a number of other races in which the humanoids, as you call them, are in that range. Creator loves variety, don't forget, and you will encounter very large beings in your space travels and very tiny ones too.

What size do the reptilians reach?

In that same range as the race of cyclops — very near fourteen to fifteen feet, as I am adjusting for your height measurements.

What other shapes do they have besides humanoid?

An enormous variety, too numerous to list here, but look around you at the reptilians you have on Earth and you'll get an idea of the variety there are.

Are there any ETs out there with the appearance of the xenomorph creature in the Alien movie?

No. Certainly, there are some really different-looking insect beings, but none as hideous — at least that we've discovered so far — as the one portrayed in the film. This creature was concocted to scare people in a movie theater and has little basis in fact.

Do you have a supervisor, committee, or council that you report to?

Yes, we have discussed this a little in the past. I normally report to a sort of council, but I also make the findings of my visits public to other planets and galaxies and even universes. Any of our citizens may read the reports and view what you call videos of these planets. That's my job — to disseminate this information for all to see.

So I may report to a council or committee, using your terms, but I don't actually have a supervisor whom I must report to and work directly for, as you meant. Our structure of government is quite open and gentle. This information is shared with our spiritual leaders, as they like to be able to view or learn or see anything we do on demand, you would say. They really do not have to ask for it, as it is there — the information, I mean — on their viewing screens.

Antura, please explain more about the wispy beings that are sometimes seen and even photographed in space — the ones who have the appearance of wispy clouds.

Yes, these are actual beings who spread themselves over several focuses or dimensions. They are souls, but their interests are in experiencing this space, this substance, which your scientists will discover and learn about in the coming years. Each soul has its interests, and they have theirs.

So do you communicate with them or just leave them alone to their own pursuits?

There you have it. We can communicate with them, but they have little interest in our affairs and we have little interest in theirs, unless we need to ask a question.

Can you tell me what percentage of the universe is made up of humanoids?

Yes, certainly a good percentage.

Is it above 35 percent?

Yes, a little higher. Forty percent would be fairly accurate.

Were humanoids created by one society?

This is a little like the chicken and the egg theory. When Creator created this universe, calls went out and several humanoid societies responded. Naturally, from them grew the large percentage of the universe you have now, you see. So to answer your question, it was not just one society but a few.

Antura, do any humanoids have hearing or a sense of smell similar to a dog's on Earth?

Yes, there are humanoid species with the ability to hear and smell as well as a dog on Earth is capable of doing. The two abilities may not exist in the same humanoid species, but there are humanoids who have great hearing and others with a great sense of smell.

What about humanoids with great eyesight, such as an eagle on Earth has?

Again, the same answer. There are many humanoids with better vision than the Earth human. Humans would actually be in the lower quadrant, shall we call it, in vision acuity.

Is there a race of people who appear like the main character in the Hellboy II *movie?*

Not exactly, but certainly there are humanoids with horns in the universe.

Do beings from different species, races, or planets ever fall in love and live together?

Yes, there are times, but the differences can be so extreme that it is a little rare for this to occur. There is more a friendship and an honoring, as compared to the actual love of taking another being as a mate.

How populated are the planets that dogs, cats, and cows originated from, and where are they located?

These planets are generally fairly populated but not overrun with these beings. There are a few million on each planet, and yes, they do tend to live fairly long lives there and do not really look quite the same, as you'll see. They were asked by the Creator's emissaries to take part in the Earth Experiment, and as I've said before, I've never known anyone to turn down a request from the Creator.

Where are their planets located?

They are spread out in different star systems. They did not originate from, say, the same spot in the sky. I will leave some things to be discovered by your explorers and scientists.

What do the dogs and cats look like on their home planets, and are they from the same soul group?

Contrary to what you have read, dogs and cats come from separate soul groups — each has a distinctive mindset, shall we call it. They certainly balance each other. Regarding their appearance, cats certainly have a feline appearance but are humanoids, along with the dogs. Again, dogs have aspects in their personalities you can recognize. You might say, "I recognize that personality from somewhere," if you are not aware of who they are.

Antura, do any planets have as large a population as does Earth, or would this be like comparing apples and oranges, since there is such a variety of life around our universe that we cannot begin to fathom yet?

In our experience, by limiting the discussion to humanoids, Earth has by far the largest population. Starting next year, Gaia will make adjustments, as you know, to reduce the population a little, but the major reduction will come from rules and laws your countries implement in the coming years to make it a priority to have fewer children.

What is the next most populated humanoid planet, Antura?

I would have to say its population is less than half of Earth's and possibly only one-third. And I might add that this planet is much larger than Earth, so keep in mind that size does make a difference in this instance.

Then would a planet with intelligent insect species be off the chart in numbers, or are there planets with other types of beings who would be quite large in population?

The intelligent insect species can be quite large, but then their sizes can be much smaller than a humanoid species. And we must not forget the reptilians, who can really proliferate with the laying of eggs rather than womb births. So again, there is so much variety out there that it is difficult to give you the short answer needed for your newsletter and book, but feel free to visit this topic again and we will cover more species.

What percentage of the universe has vegetation of some sort or another?

Easily 90 percent, although you would not recognize it as such on planets that are, say, more gaseous in nature.

That seems rather high. Did I receive this number correctly?

Yes. Again, you have much to learn about plants and plant organisms. A planet that might appear barren to you on the surface might be teeming with life below its surface, and some plant species are tiny in comparison to what you think of as a plant.

The Lyrans and Vegans

There are galaxies reported by our astronomers as being 13 billion years old. Is that an accurate statement? If so, were there intelligent societies created at that time?

Certainly they were created within a fairly short time period after the creation of their galaxies. Again, we must take into consideration your measurement of time and how inaccurate it is for dealing with universal issues. But to answer your question, yes, there have been societies that are well over 1 billion Earth years. That's where you come in — to move everyone forward to raise their vibrational levels.

Are any of these societies as old as 10 billion years?

Yes, believe it or not, there are a couple of societies even older — not quite dating back to the beginning of this universe but certainly within a few million years of it. Truly ancient by any standard, you could say.

Do they still operate on the fifth focus?

Yes, although as you may have guessed, many of these societies — or I should say the oldest ones — also operate in higher focuses too.

Would the Lyrans be one of the oldest societies?

Quite so. They are a very ancient society.

Are the Vegans also over 10 billion years old as a society?

Yes, quite so. There you have the two oldest societies in the universe. There are a couple of others that are quite old, but these two are the oldest.

Did the Lyrans begat the Pleiadians and did the Vegans begat the Sirians?

In a simplified way, yes, the Lyrans are the forefathers of several races in the Pleiades and the Vegans the same for certain societies of our Sirius system of planets. We are talking billions of years here. And yes, to answer your next question, our amphibian society is a mere child in age compared to the Lyrans, Vegans, and even the rest of the Sirian societies. But Creator recognized we would eventually make a contribution to help everyone across the universe. We are catalysts, you might say, as the Explorer Race certainly is.

Why do the Lyrans and Vegans operate on more than one focus?

A deep question, that one. Because there are those in their societies who were able to raise their vibrational levels to a point at which it was more comfortable to experience life as lightbeings — or very close to that, shall we say.

How many millions of Lyrans are there in the fifth focus?

Quite a few million — well over 100 million.

Over 200 million?

Quite so. Needless to say, in 13 billion years, they have been able to expand as far as they wished, populate as many planets as they wished, and created as many different types of people as they wished.

Does the Federation have relationships with these societies, or are you left pretty much to your own? Do they send representatives, or are they somehow involved with the Federation?

Good question. No, we do have friendly relations with both societies. They certainly are looking on the Earth Experiment with great anticipation, as we all are.

During the Star Wars with the reptilians, did the Lyrans give you assistance, or did they sit back and say, "This is not our fight"?

Much more the latter. They did attempt to mediate the situation, but we were finally able to come to a peaceful solution ourselves.

Why didn't the reptilians attack the Lyrans too?

That would have caused the reptilians a great many problems, as the Lyrans are far beyond them in development. I'll add that the Lyrans are far beyond our development as well. The reptilians knew the Lyrans would not interfere as long as they were not personally attacked, you see.

Globular Star Cluster

Antura, what is the globular cluster of 100,000 stars known as cluster M13 that the Hubble telescope took a photo of?

That is a unique cluster of stars. There are many planets revolving around those stars, as I'm sure you can appreciate. There is a unique magnetic force that holds all of these stars together.

Have you or your people visited this cluster of stars?

Oh, yes. And to answer your anticipated question whether any of the planets there are members of the Federation: No, they are too distant. As you can imagine, they have their own Federation of planets within that cluster, as their wants and needs are similar in nature. It would take hours to describe how unique this cluster of planets is, but suffice to say that you will discover many more globular clusters of stars in this universe, as the Creator loves variety.

Did you find humanoids in that star cluster?

Not so many. Again, they are quite unique, and the life forms we found there are unique too.

I'm not sure if I'm asking this correctly. Have you visited other galaxies in the universe, or do you consider these galaxies other universes themselves?

A splendid question! We do consider these galaxies, as you call them, and not separate universes. And yes, I have visited them on occasion.

Why wouldn't you spend more time visiting them instead of going to another universe?

That's such a deep question. We certainly had things we wanted to know, and sometimes that information can be best obtained not in your own schoolyard, let's say, but somewhere a long distance away.

■●CHAPTER 20●■

OTHER UNIVERSES

Have you ever visited another universe created by another creator?

Oh, yes. Several times. It is not that hard after you reach our level of progress.

When you visited another universe, was it to study a culture, or were you there as part of a delegation meeting with representatives of a planet or federation?

We wanted to see how other universes were created and for what purpose. I was there as part of a delegation, as it was known there were water planets there. Certainly that is my expertise — to work with the delegations from other water worlds.

It was quite a busy time as we communicated with each other about our differences and similarities. Certainly sometimes the differences are so great that it is almost impossible to relate, but that's what such voyages attempt to accomplish — to understanding one another and to set up future communication.

When you visited other universes, did they have galaxies and star systems similar to what the Creator of this universe made?

Yes, similar but different. It would take a very long discussion to go over the many differences, but some of the universes are quite a bit smaller than this one — easy to navigate around, shall we say, but quite interesting. One universe that I'm sending you an image of was just one big enormous galaxy with millions and billions of star systems and truly unique people or beings inhabiting them.

We could go on and on with the differences, but yes, they are somewhat similar while completely different in other respects. Because you have not been to the stars yet, it would be difficult for me to describe all the differences. Right now you have no basis for comparison, but you will have that in the future.

Then these universes are not those far galaxies we see with the use of powerful telescopes, are they?

Actually, yes, in a way.

Cosmic Neighbors

Can we see the next closest universe in the night sky, and if so, what do we call these star systems we see?

The first answer is yes, you can see that universe situated not so far away. You think of them as specific star systems, not understanding that your night sky shows not only this universe but the one next door. That's why your scientists are puzzled by those that seem to be expanding and those that seem to be retreating.

The nearest galaxy to Earth is the Andromeda Galaxy. Would this be the one in the other universe, or would it possibly be the Sagittarius or Canis Ursa Major II?

Yes, the latter two are in the other universe. The Andromeda Galaxy is not. Yes, you received me correctly.

Is the other universe that is close by younger, older, or about the same age as our universe?

Good question. It is a little older, but not by so many years, shall we say.

What would you say is the major difference between the two?

Oh, where to begin! There are enormous differences. If you recall, I said when we visited the other universe that things were so different that it was difficult for even us to understand. Again, I point out we have been doing these explorations for a long time. To give you one difference: just the makeup of the planets there is quite different. It is hard to describe when your understanding and knowledge is so limited, but take my word for it, they are different.

Antura, astronomers have discovered a large quasar group 4 billion light-years from Earth. Is this part of our universe or another?

Another, as you were guessing. With billions of other universes, one has to consider the possibility of a few of them being within the proximity of our universe. In the coming years, astronomers and scientists will narrow their definition of our universe as they recognize the possibility of other creations. They will see they are nowhere similar to this one and work on different dynamics — different laws.

CHAPTER 21

MOVING A PLANET

Antura, has the Federation of Planets ever been asked to assist societies on planets that are about to be destroyed due to collisions with other planets or stars or some planetary imbalance?

Oh, yes, several times in the past we have assisted all the beings on a given planet to move to another similar planet when their lives were threatened with extinction. Depending on the number of beings on the planet, this can be an easy transfer or a very prolonged and difficult one. We do have many large spacecraft in the Federation that can be mobilized for these instances to assist not only Federation members but also others who are not.

When the Federation finds a planet or is notified by a planetary society that their sun is in imminent danger of exploding, please go over the process of how a new planet is found to transfer the population to. How many ships must be employed, or do you just move the whole planet, an idea that just popped into my mind? Then how many ships does it take to move a planet?

Not as many as you might think. We can summon up enormous energies, and it is all done peacefully with the approval of the planet itself and those who reside there.

So do you move the planet through a portal?

Yes, most of the time we do. Again, great energies must be harnessed here to make the portal able to take on such a large object, but it can be done, and it has been done numerous times. There are beings in our Federation who have handled these circumstances several times, both in their present and past lives, which as you recall, they can draw on.

Antura, when you move a planet, how do you retain the atmosphere during the move?

An excellent question. It is retained by the enormous energy used to move the planet. It's as if the planet is wrapped in an energy cocoon during transport.

I discussed moving one planet, but in actuality, if a sun is going to explode, all the planets are in danger.

That's correct, and we will move any of the planets with life on them. Obviously, this is a huge undertaking, but it has been done countless times.

Have you had any instances when the time of moving a planet was quite close to the time of destruction, or do you always have enough warning in order to take action in a timely fashion?

It is quite rare that we will have little time, but certainly it has happened. In those cases, more resources and people are brought in to speed up the process.

Antura, was Earth moved from the Sirius B star system to its present location in this solar system?

Yes. It was decided that you could not do the Earth Experiment properly if there were dozens of spaceships flying around all the time, which was the case; plus a special planet was needed with both oceans and landmasses. You needed to be in a remote location rotating around a single sun.

So was Gaia the soul of the planet at that time?

Another good question. No, she was not. Again, a special soul was needed, so the soul of Earth at that time moved on to another young planet and Gaia took over this one.

Saturn's Moon Iapetus

Antura, my guardian angel says Saturn's moon Iapetus is artificial and was placed there over a billion years ago. Was this moon placed there by a member of the Federation or another society, such as the Lyrans or Vegans?

No, it was not done by those two societies, but that is an interesting premise. It was placed there by one of your forefathers. It was not my people, obviously, as we're not that old.

But I thought 18 to 20 million years would have been closer?

Not at all. That's when your soul groups decided to settle in the Sirius B star system. Life elsewhere had been going on for millions and millions of years before that. When Creator created this universe, he also created beings shortly thereafter.

Why would they have chosen to put a satellite around Saturn? That's just one planet out of billions out there. Are their millions of these artificial moons for other planets?

No. The society that placed it there was told by Creator to do it for the future of this planetary system and especially for the Explorer Race. Creator wanted them to work far in advance, as the rings had to be regulated that long ago so that you would have the conditions you do now.

Is this billion-year-old society part of the Federation?

No, but they are friendly neighbors, we will call them. They certainly have an interest in the Explorer Race, just as we do.

Antura, I was asked if the rings of Saturn were created by ETs, and if so, for what purpose?

They were not so much created, but as they do play a part in your development, they are kept in good working order. You will find thousands of other planets with rings when you begin to travel. The artificial moon assists in keeping the rings of Saturn to remain in their positions.

What is much more difficult is the understanding of why these rings are necessary. That's something for your scientists to ponder. It will not be solved for several hundred years. Let's leave it as one of those unexplained mysteries for those who come after you to solve. Certainly it is much more than to look pretty and different from the other planets.

CHAPTER 22

THE
FUTURE

Do you know all your next lives coming up?
For the most part, yes, but I don't dwell on that.

Will you have an Earth life after this one or continue with lives on your planet?
I will have another Earth life but not for some time.

Do you know just about when you will transition?
Quite so. Again, this is not something to dwell on, but even humans can sense long in advance of when they will transition — it's just that you hide it under a rock. We do not have multiple transition times as you do. There is no need, again, as we are not veiled and remain on our soul plan.

I do not see too many forecasts of changes after those years you list as visits. Why is that?
There will be many discussions, and we will explain great knowledge about your past to you. As far as your daily lives will go, there are not going to be any great advances in technology. Therefore, the changes will be more of an understanding of your past and what your future potentials are. It will give you direction, but we will not direct you — only explain where you fit in this great experiment.

How will science-fiction films change after first contact?
There will be great changes, since the storylines will adapt to your actual history and the history of this Federation and universe. In the films you will make about being on a mothership, the beings onboard will be created through CGI. Naturally, there will be a great desire to see these documentaries all over the world. That we're sure of.

Tom's Return
Antura, how long ago was my last life on your planet, and how many of your years did I live?

It has been a few hundred years since you were last incarnated here, so there is great anticipation of your next arrival. I know that is hard to understand from your point of view, but in the past, you have brought great change to the planet and even to the universe. You'll see. That's why your return is looked on with great anticipation.

You are coming to help us deal with the earthlings, and at the same time, you will be of great service to our communities with your wisdom — not only your wisdom from your many sojourns on Earth, but also from your thousands of lives on our planet. You were one of the first to come to this planet, just as you were one of the first to have a life on Earth.

How many years did I live?

A good number, well over 1,200 years — more on the order of 1,400 years.

When I'm born on your planet this coming round, what sort of life am I supposed to have?

An interesting question. I can't give you a lot of information yet, but I will in the future. You will be a grand master of sorts. I know that does not have any meaning to you yet, but your life will be very important for changes that need to be made here. As you know, you always act as a catalyst. You've even seen that in your earlier days: You bring change wherever you land.

Antura, how old will you be when I am birthed on the planet?

Not too much older in terms of our years. More on the order of 500 or a little more, perhaps.

Will you be my father?

No, I will not. I will be a close family friend who will see that your instruction and learning will proceed in a fast manner so that you can begin your work at a fairly early age.

No play time for me, huh?

No, there will be plenty of time, but you will be aware of why you are there and the things you need to accomplish.

Working with Negativity

Antura, where does the negativity come from since you've said all the other societies have pushed it away?

Because you are veiled, you have no way to sweep it away or any of the other terms we can use to describe something almost indescribable to you. The negativity is simply allowed to happen. In fact, you attract it to yourselves planet-wide. Those who oversee the Earth Experiment know how much you can live with. Currently, that amount is beginning to decline, as you have handled the maximum amount and still raised your overall vibrational level — quite remarkable.

Will we be working with any negative energy?

Yes, to a certain extent. Not nearly the amount we worked with on Earth but a little. You will need to assist our people in moving forward in preparation for the arrival of the earthlings, shall we call them. You will be able to relate to them much more easily than most of the population here, having lived so many lives on Earth. You will be a great asset in this regard. You will also have work with our people too. It will be quite an active and productive life, I assure you.

Why, when you know earthlings will introduce small amounts of negativity in the future, would you not go ahead and do this yourselves?

Good question. As we have never done this before, all our societies are keeping it hidden away — this negativity — until we are forced to confront it by you earthlings. By the time you are able to travel to the stars, you will have learned much about negativity and will know what each society needs to kick-start their own programs.

As you know nothing about our societies, I will tell you that introducing games and such is a delicate affair and must be handled with kid gloves — at least that's what all the societies in the Federation firmly believe. Naturally, they want to believe this to delay as long as possible the inevitable result.

Our Space Explorations

Antura, what type of life will we find on Venus and Mars, if any?

There is life on both those planets, but it is on a more cellular basis; there are no physical beings you can interact with. You will learn much from your studies of both planets. There are billions of other planets in the universe just like Mars and Venus. Your studies of both will come in handy when you go out to the stars yourselves.

Will there be any connection of the mission to the asteroid Ceres and the first contact with the Pleiadians?

Not at all. That mission will certainly be allowed to continue, as it will let you learn more about your solar system. You will have various missions over the next few hundred years as you explore more and more of this solar system and actually have colonies not only on Mars and the Moon but elsewhere as well.

Why would the Creator, the Federation, or other societies want the rings of Saturn to be in good working order for us?

You will find — your scientists of the future — that when you begin to explore the solar system, the rings play an important role. I can't say any more, as it would be a spoiler, as you say, and would not allow your scientists to have those "wow!" moments.

I just read a channeling that said the first 100 societies we meet in our space travels or contacts will be comprised of beings very similar to animals we know on Earth. Would you say that is accurate? I don't see any animal that would represent your species.

It might not appear that way, but yes, that is a fairly accurate statement. Most of the beings you will meet already have their ambassadors, shall we say, living lives on Earth so that you will not be so surprised when you meet them in the future.

Including bird men?

Oh yes, quite so — but obviously quite different from the actual birds you have on your planet. Again, there are characteristics that you will notice — birds, reptiles, ants, and mammals of many types. They are all out there but in different forms. They will not look exactly like they do on Earth. They just want you to understand their flavor, attitudes, and characteristics in a subliminal way.

Antura, would you say that virtually no society in the universe has disabled beings, as Earth does, or can that be said just for advanced societies?

While there have not been advancements made in other places to the extent of what has taken place on Earth, there can be accidents and disabilities until these societies learn or are taught how to correct them. So you cannot make a general statement about this except in the case of the advanced societies who learned how to correct disabilities millions of years ago. By the time you reach the stars, you will be able to assist societies that are behind you in development to learn how to treat these disabilities.

Is the newfound planet inhabited?

Quite so, but again it is just one of billions of planets. The beings located there are not really taking part in all this. This will remain one of your explorations for the future; one day you will discover exactly who and what they are.

Antura does the planet GJ667Cc, recently discovered by our scientists, actually have sentient life?

Yes. It is one of those planets that has not risen to the level of your planet. This will happen fairly far into the future for its inhabitants. You will find there are many planets like that, so you will treat them with a kind heart.

What are the rod-shaped objects in space recorded on video and photographs? Are they ships of some kind or living beings or a mixture of both?

Good question. Yes, for the most part, these are living beings. There are even larger ones who can be seen in the sky, but they are not spacecraft. I am not allowed to say too much about them, as they are being studied by scientists and other interested people. I will say that they are able to travel between dimensions. You will find them fascinating to study — by that I mean your scientists.

Will we be able to explore the universe with our minds — through techniques such as remote viewing — in the fifth focus?

You will find it easier to connect with those from your home planet in the fifth focus, and they will be able to feed you images much more easily than you can receive now in the denser third focus. But it will be some time before people are able to tune in at a moment's notice to a particular location in the galaxy and obtain detailed or even fragmented information on a solar system or planets within the solar system. I won't say it is not possible, but it will be something that a person would have to really want to do and then put in the practice to achieve it. There will be such individuals, but they will be few and far between, as you say.

Earth Systems

I have been told by my guardian angel that we will adopt a twelve-based number system. Is that correct?

Yes, to a point. Your number systems will not work with the mathematical systems of the universe.

Are our mathematicians aware of this system, is it something you will show us, or will we have to figure it out ourselves?

We may be allowed to show this to your scientists, as it only points in a direction and does not solve problems for them. And no, you do not have this system yet. It has been theorized by very few mathematicians on Earth who were being inspired.

Is it a system in which zeros are treated as numbers?

Yes, but your mathematicians will learn much more about this in the fairly near future. As you do not have the background, we would be completely mired down. I know this answer has been given before, but trust me, even I am not that involved in the mathematical system used. It is for those whose interests lie in that direction.

Antura, how does universal time differ from Earth time?

Our time is not built on the rotation of Earth. Millions of years ago, they created a system of measuring time in the whole universe — not just one planet. Even on Earth, you have more than one system for measuring the days, weeks, months, and years. That does not happen with universal time. It is actually much slower than Earth time. You are presently — and will continue to be — influenced by your Earth's rotation. When you go out to the stars and even to other planets, you will have to adapt to the universal time measurement or things will seem quite confusing to you.

Would you say that Earth time is two, five, or ten times faster than universal time? Or can they not be compared at all?

Universal time is much slower than the artificial time you have here on Earth. Certainly, it would be a difference of ten times or more. Is there any reason Earth people should not feel rushed? Time just flies by for you. So that comparison is fairly accurate. Naturally, this was done so that Earth humans could speed up their development.

What may appear to have taken 1,500 years on Earth actually would have been only 150 years or so in universal time. And that's why it will continue even after you begin to explore the universe. This is a little difficult to explain, as you can imagine. When you go to space, you will begin experiencing universal time as you move away from Earth, but Earth will remain in this loop of time created for the Earth Experiment. Time was sped up so that you could learn to make these quick decisions and advance at a rapid rate while handling massive amounts of negativity at the same time. The whole universe and even other universes are amazed at how you've adapted and overcome such great barriers.

I can look back and see how you have brought me along at more or less a steady rate of revealing what was going to occur, Antura. Do we still have more major revelations to go?

No, not really. You have the whole concept of what we wish to accomplish before you now. Certainly there are more questions you will think of to ask, but we have the core of the project ready, and soon you will share it with a much wider audience.

CHAPTER 23

CONCLUSION

I believe we're in for some exciting times during the next four years. Will these events all take place on time? I don't know, as I'm just the messenger passing along what I've been told.

I also wish to remind you that no one who does this work is perfect, I've been told. My reception is around 80 to 90 percent, so I know there will be corrections made in the future, since it will become easier and easier for me and everyone who wishes to try this as we settle into the fifth focus.

Just before I turned over my manuscript to my editor on February 1, 2013, I asked the following questions.

Antura, do the 2015 and 2017 dates still hold for the arrival of the Pleiadians and then your Sirian group?

Absolutely. Those dates are pretty solid now. I would say the probability is now 90 percent. Earth continues to progress, and we are excited — even more than you are — that our mission will in fact take place. It hasn't always been an absolute certainty, especially back during the time we first spoke, but each year that probability has risen.

What about for later in 2013 for the Russian announcement? I have found in the past that these dates can really slide for humans.

Yes, but we think it will still be this year. There is some contact going on now to explain the advantages of being the first.

Will I ever meet you again in this life after our visit to the mothership?

Perhaps. There have been discussions regarding you acting as sort of a liaison or ambassador to assist the contact team in meeting with not only governments and scientists to ease their trepidations in coming to meet with us but other grassroots contactees as well. We would like to see the reactions to your visit and the documentaries you will release in the following year or two. I'm sure you will volunteer if needed.

Has the number of crewmembers been solidified?

Quite so. The number will be close to 850, as there are now others who see the significance of this particular mission and wish to be part of it.

Of course. So, as we say on Earth, "May the force be with you!"

[Author's Note: If you wish to read more questions asked after this book was finalized, please go to my website www.ETConversations.com, where all my weekly newsletters are archived. You can sign up to receive them if you wish.]

GLOSSARY

Alcyone
Considered by many sources to be the Central Sun of our galaxy.

Alpha level
The level in meditation at which questions can be asked and thought-packet answers can be received.

Amphibian
A being who can live both in the ocean and on dry land.

Bosnian Pyramids
The oldest known pyramids in the world, carbon-dated to 26,000 years ago. Its Pyramid of the Sun is one-third larger than the Giza pyramid in Egypt. It is located 19 miles (30 kilometers) from the capital city Sarajevo.

Channeling
Communicating with a spiritual entity or another person or being anywhere in the universe.

Creator
The being who created this universe. There are billions of other creators, but this one is special, having designed a plan to use negative energy — something no other universe has been able to accomplish.

Cyclops
One-eyed humanoids from half the size of an average human to twice the size.

Earth Directive
Created by the Federation of Planets to prevent abductions and interference by any planetary society.

Earth Experiment
An experiment set up by Creator and our souls in which we are veiled from knowing about our souls and past lives in order to reinvent everything and work with negativity, which no society in the universe has been able to do in millions of years.

ET
Short for extraterrestrial; a being from another world.

Explorer Race
The souls taking part in the Earth Experiment.

Fast track
Souls who volunteered for the Earth Experiment are on the fast track, which enables them to raise their vibrational levels much faster than they could through lives on other planets.

The Federation of Planets
Often shortened to just the Federation. A group of 200 planets in this quadrant of the Milky Way Galaxy formed for trade and protection after the Star Wars.

Fifth focus
The fifth dimension.

Force field device
A device worn by ETs to protect them from any environment.

Gaia
The soul of Earth. Every planet and sun in the universe has a soul running things.

Golden lightbeing
See guardian angel.

Guardian angel
A whole soul, also known as a golden lightbeing due to the golden light it ema-
nates after raising its vibrational level. There are a little over one million of these
golden lightbeings who have volunteered to take care of all the souls having lives
on Earth due to the difficulty of their lives of being veiled. They prefer the name
"servants of the Creator."

Humanoids
Beings typically having two arms and two legs.

Kryon
A spiritual being channeled by Lee Carroll.

Lois J. Wetzel
Author of *Akashic Records*.

Lyrans
One of the two oldest societies in the universe; they are between 10 billion to 13
billion years old.

Most benevolent outcomes (MBOs)
A simple yet very powerful spiritual tool through which one makes requests for
everything from the mundane to the most important matters.

Mothership
Giant spaceships one mile (1.6 kilometers) in length with crews of up to 1,000
beings. They also carry smaller craft for exploration of planets.

Nibiru
A planet that intersects our solar system every 3,600 years. Nibiruans have report-
edly used earthlings for their mining operations.

Portals
The entrances to the mysterious folds in space allowing spacecraft to transit from
one part of the universe to another and even to other universes.

Portal hopping
Using multiple portals to travel to destinations across the universe.

Reptilians
The race of beings who instigated Star Wars.

Robert Shapiro
A trance channel and the author of *The Explorer Race* books and many others (Light Technology Publishing).

Scout craft
The smaller spaceships carried inside a mothership and used to explore planetary systems.

Sirius B star system
The star system where Antura's planet is located, about 500 light-years from Earth.

Soul cluster
A group of typically six to twelve soul fragments living on Earth as part of the Earth Experiment.

Soul fragments
Parts of a whole soul living on Earth.

Stargate
See portal.

Star wars
A massive war that took place millions of years ago between the reptilian race and an amalgamation of planets in the Milky Way Galaxy.

Theo
The name the author uses for his guardian angel — one of a little over one million golden lightbeings who oversee the lives of all the soul fragments living on Earth.

Third focus
The third dimension.

Thought packets
What Tom's guardian angel says he, Antura, and others send and we download from the right side of our brains to the left.

Time loop
This refers to a time-space continuum set up for the Earth Experiment so that souls can live simultaneously in the past, present, and future.

Timelines
The twelve parallel worlds created for our souls' greatest learning from each Earth life. See chapter 8 for a more detailed explanation.

Translation device
Part of the force field device, this unit is able to translate every language in the universe using brain waves, sounds, and so forth. The being using the translation device hears all others' words in his or her own language.

Tripping out
Going deeper into the theta level during meditation to the point at which it becomes very difficult, if not impossible, to ask questions and receive thought-packet answers.

UFO
Unidentified flying object — quite often a scout craft from a mothership.

Universal years
These are much slower than Earth years — perhaps at a ratio of one for every ten Earth years.

Vegans
One of the two oldest societies in the universe, they are 10 to 13 billion years old.

Veiled
The condition Earth humans have that prevents them from knowing about their soul experiences on other planets and even previous lives on Earth as part of the Earth Experiment. This veil is both a mental and spiritual barrier.

ABOUT THE
AUTHOR

TOM T. MOORE is the author of *The Gentle Way* books, a speaker, and a frequent radio guest. For the past twenty-five years, he has worked as the president and CEO of his own international motion picture and TV program distribution business based in Dallas-Fort Worth Metroplex, Texas. During this time, he has traveled extensively as part of his business duties to international film markets held in Cannes, France; Milan, Italy; Los Angeles, California; and Budapest, Hungary. Tom was inspired to publicize the modality of the Gentle Way, which dates back to Atlantean times and is described as a giant step forward over the law of attraction. He says that requesting benevolent outcomes for the past fifteen years has resulted in leading a gentler, less stressful, and less fearful life — the Gently Way!

Before becoming an international film distributor, Tom owned and operated an international wholesale tour company with his wife, selling tours through 3,000 travel agents nationwide. That business began out of his first successful venture, a ski club for single adults, which grew to be the largest snow ski club in Texas. Tom is still an avid skier and loves to ski in the United States, Canada, and Europe.

Tom graduated with a BBA in finance from Texas Christian University in Fort Worth, Texas, and served in the U.S. Army as a first lieutenant. He is a native of Dallas, Texas, and is married with two children.

Tom publishes a weekly newsletter and blog, and his articles have appeared in a number of international and regional magazines. You can read his monthly column in the *Sedona Journal of Emergence!* To book Tom T. Moore as a speaker at your next conference or event, email him at speaker@TheGentleWayBook.com.

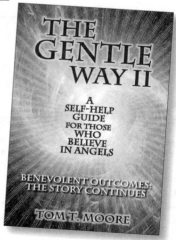

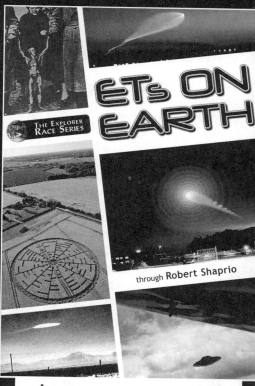

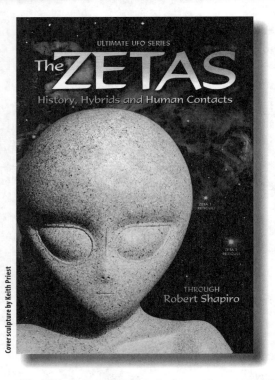

Shamanic Secrets Mastery Series

Speaks of Many Truths and Reveals the Mysteries through Robert Shapiro

This book explores the heart and soul connection between humans and Earth. Through that intimacy, miracles of healing and expanded awareness can flourish. To heal the planet and be healed as well, we can lovingly extend our energy selves out to the mountains and rivers and intimately bond with Earth. Gestures and vision can activate our hearts to return us to a healthy, caring relationship with the land we live on. The character of some of Earth's most powerful features is explored and understood with exercises given to connect us with those places. As we project our love and healing energy there, we help Earth to heal from human destruction of the planet and its atmosphere. Dozens of photographs, maps, and drawings assist the process in twenty-five chapters, which cover Earth's more critical locations.

498 PP. **$19.95 ISBN 978-1-891824-12-8**

Learn to understand the sacred nature of your own physical body and some of the magnificent gifts it offers you. When you work with your physical body in these new ways, you will discover not only its sacredness but also how it is compatible with Mother Earth, the animals, the plants, and even the nearby planets, all of which you now recognize as being sacred in nature. It is important to feel the value of oneself physically before you can have any lasting physical impact on the world. If a physical energy does not feel good about itself, it will usually be resolved; other physical or spiritual energies will dissolve it because they are unnatural.

The better you feel about your physical self when you do the work in the previous book, as well as this one and the one to follow, the greater and more lasting will be the benevolent effect on your life, on the lives of those around you, and ultimately on your planet and universe.

544 PP. **$25.00 ISBN 978-1-891824-29-6**

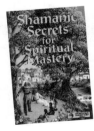

Spiritual mastery encompasses many different means to assimilate and be assimilated by the wisdom, feelings, flow, warmth, function, and application of all beings in your world that you will actually contact in some way. A lot of spiritual mastery has been covered in different bits and pieces throughout all the books we've done. My approach to spiritual mastery, though, will be as grounded as possible in things that people on Earth can use — but it won't include the broad spectrum of spiritual mastery, like levitation and invisibility. I'm trying to teach you things that you can actually use and benefit from. My life is basically going to represent your needs, and it gets out the secrets that have been held back in a storylike fashion so that it is more interesting."

— Speaks of Many Truths through Robert Shapiro
676 PP. **$29.95 ISBN 978-1-891824-58-6**

Zoosh and His Friends through Robert Shapiro

❼ EXPLORER RACE: COUNCIL of CREATORS

The thirteen core members of the Council of Creators discuss their adventures in coming to awareness of themselves and their journeys on the way to the Council on this level. They discuss the advice and oversight they offer to all creators, including the Creator of this local universe. These beings are wise, witty, and joyous, and their stories of Love's Creation create an expansion of our concepts as we realize that we live in an expanded, multiple-level reality.

273 PP. $14.95 ISBN 13: 978-1-891824-13-5

❽ EXPLORER RACE and ISIS

This is an amazing book! It has priestess training, shamanic training, Isis's adventures with Explorer Race beings — before Earth and on Earth — and an incredibly expanded explanation of the dynamics of the Explorer Race. Isis is the prototypal loving, nurturing, guiding feminine being, the focus of feminine energy. She has the ability to expand limited thinking without making people with limited beliefs feel uncomfortable. She is a fantastic storyteller, and all of her stories are teaching stories. If you care about who you are, why you are here, where you are going and what life is all about—pick up this book. You won't lay it down until you are through, and then you will want more.

304 PP. $14.95 ISBN 13: 978-1-891824-11-1

❾ EXPLORER RACE and JESUS

The core personality of that being known on Earth as Jesus, along with his students and friends, describes with clarity and love his life and teaching 2,000 years ago. He states that his teaching is for all people of all races in all countries. Jesus announces here for the first time that he and two others, Buddha and Mohammed, will return to Earth from their place of being in the near future, and a fourth being, a child already born now on Earth, will become a teacher and prepare humanity for their return. So heartwarming and interesting, you won't want to put it down.

327 PP. $16.95 ISBN 13: 978-1-891824-14-2

❿ EXPLORER RACE: EARTH HISTORY and LOST CIVILIZATIONS

Speaks of Many Truths and Zoosh, through Robert Shapiro, explain that planet Earth, the only water planet in this solar system, is on loan from Sirius as a home and school for humanity, the Explorer Race. Earth's recorded history goes back only a few thousand years, its archaeological history a few thousand more. Now this book opens up as if a light was on in the darkness, and we see the incredible panorama of brave souls coming from other planets to settle on different parts of Earth. We watch the origins of tribal groups and the rise and fall of civilizations, and we can begin to understand the source of the wondrous diversity of plants, animals, and humans that we enjoy here on beautiful Mother Earth.

310 PP $14.95 ISBN 13: 978-1-891824-20-3

⓫ EXPLORER RACE: ET VISITORS SPEAK

Even as you are searching the sky for extraterrestrials and their spaceships, ETs are here on planet Earth—they are stranded, visiting, exploring, studying the culture, healing Earth of trauma brought on by irresponsible mining, or researching the history of Christianity over the past 2,000 years. Some are in human guise, and some are in spirit form. Some look like what we call animals as they come from the species' home planet and interact with their fellow beings — those beings who we have labeled cats or cows or elephants. Some are brilliant cosmic mathematicians with a sense of humor; they are presently living here as penguins. Some are fledgling diplomats training for future postings on Earth when we have ET embassies here. In this book, these fascinating beings share their thoughts, origins, and purposes for being here. 340 PP. $14.95 ISBN 13: 978-1-891824-28-9

⓬ EXPLORER RACE: TECHNIQUES for GENERATING SAFETY

Wouldn't you like to generate safety so you could go wherever you need to go and do whatever you need to do in a benevolent, safe, and loving way for yourself? Learn safety as a radiated environment that will allow you to gently take the step into the new timeline, into a benevolent future, and away from a negative past. 177 PP. $9.95 ISBN 13: 978-1-891824-26-5

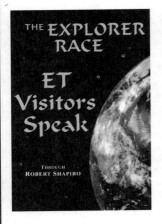

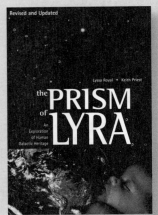

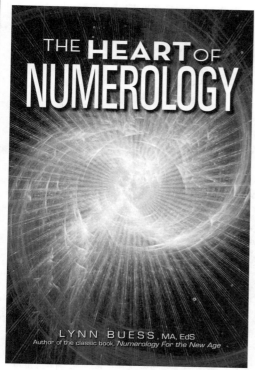

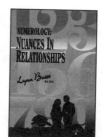

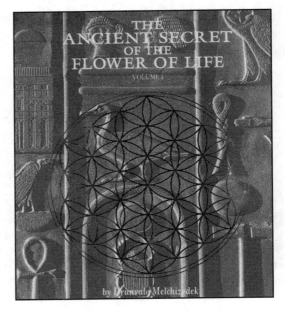

THE ANCIENT SECRET
OF THE FLOWER OF LIFE
VOLUME 2

- **The Unfolding of the Third Informational System**
- **Whispers from Our Ancient Heritage**
- **Unveiling the Mer-Ka-Ba Meditation**
- **Using Your Mer-Ka-Ba**
- **Connecting to the Levels of Self**
- **Two Cosmic Experiments**
- **What We May Expect in the Forthcoming Dimensional Shift**

$25⁰⁰ Softcover, 252 PP.
ISBN 978-1-891824-21-0

The sacred Flower of Life pattern, the primary geometric generator of all physical form, is explored in even more depth in this volume, the second half of the famed Flower of Life workshop. The proportions of the human body; the nuances of human consciousness; the sizes and distances of the stars, planets, and moons; and even the creations of humankind are all shown to reflect their origins in this beautiful and divine image. Through an intricate and detailed geometrical mapping, Drunvalo Melchizedek shows how the seemingly simple design of the Flower of Life contains the genesis of our entire third-dimensional existence.

From the pyramids and mysteries of Egypt to the new race of Indigo children, Drunvalo presents the sacred geometries of the reality and the subtle energies that shape our world. We are led through a divinely inspired labyrinth of science and stories, logic and coincidence, on a path of remembering where we come from and the wonder and magic of who we are.

Finally, for the first time in print, Drunvalo shares the instructions for the Mer-Ka-Ba meditation, step-by-step techniques for the re-creation of the energy field of the evolved human, which is the key to ascension and the next dimensional world. If done from love, this ancient process of breathing prana opens up for us a world of tantalizing possibility in this dimension, from protective powers to the healing of oneself, of others, and even of the planet.

✣ Light Technology PUBLISHING

BY DRUNVALO MELCHIZEDEK

LIVING IN THE HEART

Includes a CD with Heart Meditation

"Long ago we humans used a form of communication and sensing that did not involve the brain in any way; rather, it came from a sacred place within our hearts. What good would it do to find this place again in a world where the greatest religion is science and the logic of the mind? Don't I know this world where emotions and feelings are second-class citizens? Yes, I do. But my teachers have asked me to remind you who you really are. You are more than human being, much more. For within your heart is a place, a sacred place, where the world can literally be remade through conscious cocreation. If you give me permission, I will show you what has been shown to me."

- Beginning with the Mind
- Seeing in the Darkness
- Learning from indigenous Tribes
- The Sacred Space of the Heart
- The Unity of Heaven and Earth
- Leaving the Mind and Entering the Heart
- The Sacred Space of the Heart Meditation
- The Mer-Ka-Ba and the Sacred Space of the Heart
- Conscious Cocreation from the Heart Connected to the Mind

$25.00 Softcover, 120 PP.
ISBN 978-1-891824-43-2

Drunvalo Melchizedek's life experience reads like an encyclopedia of breakthroughs in human endeavor. He studied physics and art at the University of California at Berkeley, but he feels that his most important education came after college. In the past 25 years, he has studied with over 70 teachers from all belief systems and religious understandings. For some time now, he has been bringing his vision to the world through the Flower of Life program and the Mer-Ka-Ba meditation. This teaching encompasses every area of human understanding, explores the development of mankind from ancient civilizations to the present time, and offers clarity regarding the world's state of consciousness and what is needed for a smooth and easy transition into the 21st century.